FRENCH COUNTRY
COOKING

INTERNATIONAL GOURMET

FRENCH COUNTRY
COOKING

Eileen Reece

WARD LOCK

First published in paperback in Great Britain in 1990 by
Ward Lock Limited, Villiers House, 41/47 Strand,
London WC1N 5JE, a Cassell Company.

This edition published in 1993

Designed by Melissa Orrom.
Text filmset in Garamond Original by
M & R Computerised Typesetting Ltd.,
Grimsby.

Printed and bounded in Hong Kong by Colorcraft Ltd

ISBN 1 85079 200 3

Acknowledgements

Inside Photography by James Murphy
Home Economist – Nigel Slater
Stylist – Sarah Wiley
Line drawings by Lorraine Harrison

Notes

It is important to follow either the metric
or the imperial measures when using the
recipes in this book. Do not use a
combination of measures.

All recipes serve four people, unless
otherwise specified.

CONTENTS

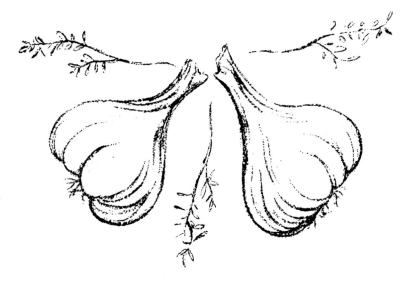

INTRODUCTION

The French farm kitchen in no way resembles its English equivalent. The farmhouse itself, issue of bitter bloodshed when land was wrenched from aristocratic possession by an exploited peasantry in the Revolution of 1789, has no gracious atmosphere. The hard driving force that acquired it still exists in running it.

The farm is, for each family, a small industry in which all its members work, male and female alike, striving side by side to enrich and enlarge the holding so hard won by their ancestors.

In Lorraine, however, and in the more remote parts of the country, beautiful farmhouses which escaped the holocaust of the Revolution still exist. But the average French farmhouse has none of the architectural beauty for which so many of our own are noted. The present trend for interior decoration has passed them by, although the one room in the house that is likely to have been improved is the kitchen. The hard-working French farmer's main concern is food, growing it, raising it and eating it. In an economy where young and old work in the fields in order to reduce expenditure to a minimum, the only money parted with willingly is for food.

Like most farmers the world over their everyday diet consists of home produce, vegetables, fruit, eggs, milk, rabbits and pork with occasional treats of chicken and game in season. Cheeses and fruit other than those the farm produces the countrywoman buys throughout the year.

This, however, does not diminish her almost obsessive sense of economy, which allows no waste whatsoever.

At the same time her culinary standards are high, and with the rational mind of her race, she knows that good food is essential to good work output. Moreover, she takes into account the fact that food is the Frenchman's daily pleasure and one that never palls.

The recipes she uses are those used by her mother and grandmother before her. But while the everyday dishes are mainly of the type that can be prepared early and left to cook by themselves while she goes about her work on the farm, on Sundays and fête days more elaborate

6

dishes are prepared, pâté or some other appetizing first course is added to the menu and a fruit tart will be served instead of fresh fruit.

Given any family event to celebrate, the humblest farm kitchen excels itself in the preparation of a gargantuan meal. Every village has its expert amateur cook for these occasions, and the country women called in 'to do the wedding' produce some of the best cooking in France. Plans for the feast are laid weeks in advance and, with the expert presiding, the women of the family spend more time discussing the menu than they do discussing their clothes. Delicacies of intricate preparation are proposed and on the great day the culinary talent displayed has to be savoured to be believed.

The abundance of national produce, the Frenchman's discriminating palate, his wife's love of cooking and the country's instinctive appreciation of good living all contribute to a gastronomic standard that has won world-wide approval. This perfection is also due to the good pans on which every French cook insists. They are often part of her heritage along with the family recipes. Made of heavy cast iron, some of them thickly enamelled, they are designed mainly for use on top of the cooker, thereby cutting fuel costs and time.

The cast-iron *Dufeu* with its sunken lid, which is filled with water to create condensation, produces meat of remarkable tenderness whose shrinkage during cooking is cut to a minimum.

The heavy iron *cocotte*, lidded and thickly enamelled, in which vegetables are cooked without water, makes their contents a most flavourful dish worthy of being served as a separate course – which it usually is. Our equivalent is a braising pot.

Gratin dishes, shallow and wide, are used for their extensive surface, which is perfect for creating the crisp brown crust essential to the success of many dishes.

All these classic pans, casseroles and dishes are still made today by Le Creuset at the Fonderies de Cousances as they first were in 1553.

The *mouli-légumes*, that economical precursor of the blender, and the *sauteuse*, a large straight-sided frying pan with a tightly fitting lid, are perhaps the favourites. In the latter vegetables and chicken are browned, herbs and wine added, the lid clamped down and the pot left unattended over low heat for 1½ hours. By then an entire main course and delicious sauce are ready to be served.

These are found in every kitchen equipment shop from Boulogne to Baton Rouge.

Notes

It is important to follow **either** the metric **or** imperial measures when using these recipes. All spoon measures are level.

Bread or breadcrumbs in all recipes should not be steam-baked. Oven-baked bread is easily obtained from small private bakeries.

Parmesan and Gruyère cheese for grating should be brought in the piece and grated as required. In this way they have more flavour and are more economical.

Curd cheese should be bought in bulk from delicatessen counters. The kind made commercially and sold in tubs is not suitable for the recipes given.

Beaten egg whites give better results when, after being beaten until stiff, they are chilled and beaten again at the time of use.

SAUCES & DRESSINGS

French cooking is world-famous for its sauces. They may appear complicated in flavour and consistency, but appearances are deceptive – they are made of very simple ingredients and prepared with an intuitive feeling for balance, a sure touch, and without fuss, every day of the week in French country kitchens. The countrywoman knows that a good sauce or dressing can be the making of a dish, and that mopping up the sauce with hard-crusted bread is one of the pleasures of eating.

Coulis de Tomates
Fresh Tomato Sauce

Makes 500ml/⅞ pint

2 × 15ml spoons/2 tablespoons olive oil
225g/8 oz onions, chopped
salt, black pepper, sugar

700g/1½ lb large ripe tomatoes, skinned and chopped
1 clove garlic, crushed
1 × 15ml spoon/1 tablespoon chopped basil

Put the olive oil into a large pan over medium heat, add the onions and mix well. Sprinkle with salt and cook until transparent. Add the tomatoes, garlic, more salt, pepper and a large pinch of sugar and cook, uncovered, until juice runs from the tomatoes.

Reduce heat, stir occasionally and allow to bubble until the liquid has been re-absorbed and the mixture is reduced to a thick purée. Stir in the basil and serve.

Notes This sauce can be bottled and sterilized or frozen. It keeps well for the winter.

If basil is not available, substitute a simple bouquet garni cooked with the tomatoes. Remove before serving.

Sauce Béchamel
Béchamel Sauce

Makes 300ml/½ pint   *Makes 600ml/1 pint*

15g/½ oz butter
2 × 5ml spoons/2 teaspoons flour
300ml/½ pint hot milk
salt, black pepper

25g/1 oz butter
1 × 15ml spoon/1 tablespoon flour
600ml/1 pint hot milk
salt, black pepper

Melt the butter in a saucepan over low heat and work in the flour with a wooden spoon. Cook for a few moments without colouring, then add the hot milk gradually, stirring until incorporated. Increase the heat to moderate and simmer for 5 minutes after boiling, stirring meanwhile, until the sauce is thick and smooth.
Season to taste.

Note If the sauce has to wait before use, cover with a piece of buttered paper pressed lightly on the surface. This will prevent a skin from forming.

Sauce aux Câpres
Caper Sauce

Makes 150ml/¼ pint (approx)

3 × 15ml spoons/3 tablespoons tarragon
   vinegar
150ml/¼ pint double cream

salt, black pepper
2 × 15ml spoons/2 tablepoons capers, drained
   and chopped

Pour the vinegar into a small stainless steel or lined saucepan and boil it down rapidly over high heat until 2.5ml/½ teaspoon remains.
Draw the pan from the heat, stir in the cream with a wooden spoon, season, and when liquid, replace the pan over low heat.
Bring to boiling and, stirring constantly, boil for 2 minutes. Add the capers and cook for 1 more minute only.

Sauce au Citron
Lemon and Herb Sauce

Makes 100ml/3½ fl oz (approx)

2.5ml/½ teaspoon salt
2 × 5ml spoons/2 teaspoons lemon juice
6 × 15ml spoons/6 tablespoons olive oil

3 × 15ml spoons/3 tablespoons chopped parsley
3 × 15ml spoons/3 tablespoons chopped chervil or tarragon

Dissolve the salt in the lemon juice, then beat in the oil until the mixture is thick and cloudy. Mix in the chopped herbs. Check the seasoning, adding a little more lemon juice if necessary.

Note Salt will not dissolve in oil, so always use lemon juice (or vinegar) first, before oil.

Mayonnaise aux Herbes
Herb Mayonnaise

Makes 225g/8 oz (approx)

1 large egg
2.5ml/½ teaspoon strong Dijon mustard
salt, black pepper
150ml/¼ pint olive or corn oil

1 × 5ml spoon/1 teaspoon wine vinegar
1 × 5ml spoon/1 teaspoon chopped chervil or parsley
1 × 15ml spoon/1 tablespoon chopped chives

Put the ingredients in a cool place several hours before making the mayonnaise. If they are all at the same temperature, there is less likelihood of the sauce separating.

Separate the egg and slide the yolk into a large soup plate, add the mustard, season and, stirring steadily with a wooden spoon, add the oil drop by drop, working it in very slowly over a wide circle. Alternatively use a blender.

When thick, add the vinegar a drop at a time, beating constantly. If the mayonnaise should fail to thicken before adding the vinegar, work in a few drops of iced water, beating vigorously meanwhile.

Add a pinch of salt to the egg white and beat to a stiff peak. *Fold* it into the mayonnaise with the chopped herbs. Do not beat or stir.

Chill until required.

Note If a blender is used it must be at the lowest pace.

11

Pestou
Garlic and Basil Dressing

Makes 200ml/⅓ pint (approx)

The most popular way of serving noodles in Provence is with pestou, a thick cream of garlic, fresh basil, Parmesan cheese and olive oil. Basil grows luxuriantly in every Mediterranean garden. It can be grown easily in an English garden or in a pot on a sunny window sill.

4 cloves garlic, chopped
2 × 15ml spoons/2 tablespoons chopped basil

100g/4 oz Parmesan cheese, grated
5–6 × 15ml spoons/5–6 tablespoons olive oil

Pound some of the cheese with the basil and garlic in a mortar with a pestle until it forms a thick cream. Continue pounding while adding the remaining cheese, then beat in the oil drop by drop as for mayonnaise. Continue beating until a thick green cream is obtained.
To serve pestou with noodles, cook and drain noodles as advised on page 42, turn them into a heated bowl, pour the pestou over and mix thoroughly. Serve immediately and hand grated Parmesan separately.

Note If a pestle and mortar are not available, the best substitute is a wooden bowl and the bottom of a small bottle. Adding a pinch of salt to the garlic makes it easier to crush to a paste.

Variation
To make pestou go further when basil is scarce, work a small handful of chopped parsley into the cheese as well.
At the same time work in 2 large tomatoes, skinned, de-seeded and finely chopped.

Vinaigrette
French Dressing

Makes 60ml/¹/₁₀ pint (approx)

*1 × 15ml spoon/1 tablespoon wine vinegar
(tarragon- or garlic-flavoured or plain)*
2.5ml/½ teaspoon salt

black pepper
3 × 15ml spoons/3 tablespoons olive oil

Pour the vinegar into a small bowl, add the salt and stir until it dissolves. Add pepper and beat in the oil gradually, until thick and cloudy.
Whatever the quantity of dressing required always use 1 part wine vinegar to 3 parts oil.

Note This quantity is sufficient to dress a salad for 4 people.

Variation
Olive oil is used when making a plain dressing, but when some flavouring is added such as chopped herbs, onions, capers or French mustard, corn oil may be used instead.
Vinaigrette can be used on all green salads.

Chapelure
Baked Breadcrumbs

Chapelure is made with stale bread or crusts baked in the bottom of the oven while it is in use for other cooking. When quite hard, dry, and golden in colour, crush with a rolling pin until fine and store the crumbs in a screw-topped jar.

HERBS & SEASONINGS

Fresh herbs are more characateristic of French country cooking than are wine and cream, which are used mainly in regions where the climate is favourable to their production.

Dried herbs lack the potency of fresh, which can be grown satisfactorily even by town dwellers who have no garden. The seeds of annuals are sown in containers filled with good loam or potting compost and placed on a sunny window sill. Perennials will flourish in small tubs placed in the sun on a balcony or terrace.

Herbs and their uses

Basil: young fresh leaves have an affinity with all tomato dishes. Fresh, they are the main ingredient of pestou (see page 12). Fresh or dried basil is used for flavouring veal, chicken and rabbit dishes. (Annual.)

Bay: the dried or fresh leaves are used to flavour soups, casseroles, pâtés and some fruit dishes, such as baked pears. The fresh leaves are very pungent. Use more sparingly than dried ones. (Perennial.)

Bergamot: the leaves make an excellent herb tea.

Borage: use fresh young leaves in salads. They give a cucumber-like flavour. Avoid using mature leaves as they are tough in texture. Also used for making herb tea, and flavouring iced drinks or claret cup. (Annual.)

Bouquet garni: this is an indispensible ingredient in French cooking. Tie together 2 large stalks of parsley, 1 small sprig thyme and/or rosemary and 1 bay leaf. Tie the end of the string to the pan handle for easy removal. This bouquet is used to flavour soups, sauces, meats, fish and vegetable dishes.

Chervil: this herb of the parsley family is only used fresh, in salads or with eggs and fish. It also makes an excellent summer soup. (Annual.)

Chives: this grass-like herb has a strong onion flavour. Make small bunches of 15–20 strands and snip with scissors directly into the eggs for an omelet, a tomato or green salad to save the trouble of peeling an onion. (Perennial.)

Dill: the feathery foliage and stalk have a great affinity with fish. (Annual.)

A selection of the herbs commonly used in French cuisine:
Left to right back row: basil, continental parsley; middle: garlic and lemon balm,
chives, mint, dill; front: marjoram, rosemary, parsley

Fennel: this herb is first cousin to dill and has a distinctive aniseed flavour. It is an important ingredient when baking a whole fish. (Perennial.)

Garlic: an aromatic bulb which should be used sparingly. A cut clove rubbed around the salad bowl will flavour it correctly – 2 skinned cloves will flavour a leg of lamb. (Annual.)

Herbes du Midi: this gives the authentic Provençal flavour to casseroles, game and fish. Bake 23g/1 oz orange peel until hard, break it into small pieces and mix with chipped nutmeg. Add dried bay leaves, wild and garden thyme, savory, lavender and rosemary, and work to a fine consistency in a blender or coffee grinder.

Juniper: the berries are used in pâtés and sauces and to flavour marinades for game. Juniper bushes, like bay trees, are very decorative. (Perennial.)

Marjoram: both annual and perennial varieties are used for flavouring soups, sauces, casseroles and pâtés.

Mint: this herb is rarely used in French cooking, but a personal discovery widely approved is to sprinkle finely chopped fresh mint on each serving of hot vegetable soup. It can also replace chopped parsley in salads. (Perennial.)

Parsley: this biennial herb is widely used fresh. It is not a satisfactory herb to use dried. The stalk is used in bouquet garni and in casseroles, and the leaves are chopped and added to omelets, salads and sauces.

Rosemary: a popular perennial herb in the French kitchen for use in casseroles, bouquet garni or any dish which needs distinctive flavouring. Either fresh or dried it has a pungent flavour and should be used sparingly. Keep a sprig of rosemary in a small bottle of olive oil to brush over lamb chops 1 hour before grilling.

Sage: little used in French cooking – and then only when fresh, to flavour pork and a few vegetable dishes. (Perennial.)

Savory: the fresh leaves are used in salads, sauces and stuffing. The flavour resembles that of thyme, but is somewhat sharper. (Annual and perennial.)

Shallots: an essential ingredient in French cooking. The flavour is reminiscent of garlic, but less pungent and rather stronger than onion. Chopped, it is used in omelets, pâtés, stuffings and sauces. (Annual.)

Sorrel: this perennial plant, part herb, part vegetable, is very popular in France. It is used raw in mixed salads and omelets. It is also used cooked in a delicious soup and as a vegetable. In this case it is used with an equal quantity of lettuce and cooked like spinach.

Tarragon: another essential herb in French cooking, used fresh to flavour salads, sauces, vegetables, fish and chicken dishes. It is important to grow the French variety (Artemesia dracunculus) and not the Russian. (Perennial.)

Thyme: used in a bouquet garni and to flavour casseroles, sauces and stuffings. Like rosemary it should be used sparingly. (Perennial.)

SOUPS

In French cooking meat or bone stock is generally made for use in sauces and casseroles. While many of the most popular soups are vegetable-based, the country cook introduces ingredients calculated to give extra nutritive value.

Her three different methods of soup-making are as follows:

Pork and vegetable soups
Belly of pork is used in these recipes, sometimes chopped finely to add to the vegetables, and sometimes cooked in one piece to be served with the vegetables as a main course. In this case the liquid is retained to be served on the side or later.

Vegetable soups
The prepared vegetables are salted and cooked slowly with butter or poultry fat in a sealed pan. This draws out the juices and full flavour of the ingredients before water is added. These soups are served either with butter stirred in, or bound with an egg yolk and cream, or poured over slices of coarse farmhouse bread. Sometimes breadcrumbs are stirred into the soup 5 minutes before serving, to act as a thickening.

Meat broths
These are made from reserved carcasses, bones and other debris of poultry and game. They are browned first to enhance the flavour, then simmered with herbs and vegetables to produce a fine-quality broth.

Garnishes

Crisply grilled bacon: crumbled over vegetable and also sorrel soup.

Baked croûtons: for country soups are made of thick wholemeal crusts, cut into thumb-sized pieces and baked hard in the oven.

Fried croûtons: are made by cutting white bread into 1cm/½ inch thick slices, removing the crust, then cutting into large cubes and frying in foaming butter until golden on all sides. Drain on absorbent paper and keep hot in the oven until served.

Herbs: can be used to give flavour and colour to soups. The favourites are chopped chervil, parsley or mint. All add greatly to vegetable soups.

Garlic: chopped finely with parsley, it makes the famous *gringot*.

Gruyère cheese and parsley: chopped and mixed together make any soup much more sustaining.

Bouillon de Poulet
Chicken Broth

Makes about 600ml/1 pint

carcass of 1 roast chicken, broken up, skin and
   debris included
15g/½ oz butter, melted
1.2 litres/2 pints cold water
1 large onion, halved

2 cloves
1 large carrot, peeled and finely sliced
1 × 5ml spoon/1 teaspoon peppercorns
1 × 5ml spoon/1 teaspoon salt
1 bouquet garni (see page 14)

Brush the pieces of carcass with melted butter and brown under a low grill until well coloured, or brown in the oven if in use.
Place in large pan with skin and other debris. Cover with water and bring to boiling point over low heat. Skim off froth as it rises and when cleared, add onion halves each stuck with a clove, carrot, peppercorns, salt and herbs.
Cover and cook slowly for 1½ hours either over low heat or in the bottom of the oven.
Remove lid, increase heat and continue simmering fast for 20 minutes, by which time the bouillon will have reduced by half.
Strain into large bowl.
Remove all fat, first with a metal cooking spoon, then by passing pieces of kitchen paper over the surface until clean.
Reheat in a clean pan and serve in small soup cups.
Freeze for other uses.

*Ingredients such as these are widely used as
garnishes for soups (pages 17–18)*

Soupe aux Coques
Cockle Soup

Serves 6

The north and west coasts of France produce splendid cockles, which are the main ingredients of a well-known soup.

40g/1½ oz butter
3 large leeks, white part only, cleaned and
 finely sliced
salt, white pepper
1 litre/1¾ pints warm water

350g/12 oz floury potatoes, finely sliced
1.2 litres/2 pints cockles, scrubbed and
 washed
2 medium sized egg yolks
4 × 15ml spoons/4 tablespoons double cream

Melt the butter in a large pan over low heat. Add the leeks and salt, cover and cook until soft, stirring occasionally. Add the warm water and potatoes, cover and simmer slowly until the potatoes can be crushed.

Put the cockles into a large pan over high heat and shake the pan until they open. As each one opens remove from the pan, remove the shell and set the cockles aside, leaving the liquor to settle. Pour it twice through a paper-lined sieve.

Reduce the vegetables and soup to purée in a blender, add cockle liquor and enough hot water to make it up to 2 litres/3½ pints. Season to taste and reduce slightly over high heat.

When ready to serve, beat the egg yolks and cream together in a bowl. Draw the pan from the heat, add a ladleful of soup gradually to the cream binding and beat well. Return this mixture to the pan *gradually*, stir in the cockles and continue until slightly thickened.

Do not boil again.

Serve immediately in well-heated bowls.

Potage aux Haricots
Haricot Bean Soup

Serves 6

225g/8 oz dried haricot beans, soaked
  overnight
2.5 litres/4 pints cold water
1 bouquet garni (see page 14)
1 large onion, halved
2 cloves
1 clove garlic, peeled

1 small head celery, washed, trimmed and
  thickly sliced
2 large leeks, thickly sliced
50g/2 oz butter
700g/1½ lb Mediterranean tomatoes,
  chopped
salt, black pepper
2 large eggs

Wash the beans in several changes of cold water. Place in a large soup pan, cover with cold water and boil for 10 minutes. Drain and wash again. Return them to the pan with quantity of water indicated, add the herbs, garlic, and onion halves each stuck with a clove. Bring slowly to boiling over low heat, then simmer for 1½ hours, until beans are almost cooked.

Soften the celery and leeks in half the butter melted in another pan, stirring occasionally. When tender, add the tomatoes. Mix, season well, cover and leave to simmer gently for 30 minutes.

Remove cloves and herbs from the other pan and add the tomato mixture. Cook for 10 minutes and pass through the mouli-légumes coarsely, or blend without reducing to a purée.

Return the soup to the pan, season well and bring back to boiling point. Soften the remaining butter to a cream, then beat in the eggs until incorporated. Proceed as for Soupe aux Coques, page 20, and serve immediately in well-heated bowls.

Note Any soup left over can be reheated in a jug standing in a deep panful of simmering water for 10 minutes and stirred occasionally.

La Trempine
Hot Wine Soup

Serves 6

Farmers and fishermen on the northern coast of France start the day with the following inspired concoction, which they say keeps out the cold. For less robust constitutions it makes an excellent nightcap.

1 large piece rye or wholemeal bread crust,
*   torn into 12*
12 large sugar lumps
200ml/6 fl oz boiling water

1 litre/1¾ pints strong red wine
1 stick cinnamon or 2 × 5 ml spoons/2
*   teaspoons powdered cinnamon*
2 × 5ml spoons/2 teaspoons sugar

Heat the oven to 140°C/275°F/Gas 1 and place 6 small earthenware bowls inside. When warm put 2 pieces of breadcrust and 2 lumps of sugar in each, divide the boiling water between them and put back in the oven.
Pour the wine into an enamel-lined saucepan, add the cinnamon and sugar and place over very low heat. *On no account must the wine boil.* When it is warm, check flavouring, allowing for the sugar in the bowls. Heat until hot when tested with a knuckle joint. Pour steaming into the bowls and serve immediately, but sparingly to the uninitiated.

Soupe à l'oignon de Poitou
Poitou Onion Soup

Serves 6

Country people in Poitou replace the grilled cheese gratinée of the Parisian's onion soup with a mixture of parsley and garlic known as *gringot*.

3 large cloves garlic, roughly chopped
4 × 15ml spoons/4 tablespoons roughly chopped parsley
12 large Spanish onions, finely chopped
75g/3 oz butter

salt, white pepper
2 × 15ml spoons/2 tablespoons plain flour
1.5 litres/2½ pints hot water
6 thin slices stale rye bread
150ml/¼ pint double cream

Chop the garlic and parsley finely together, this is the *gringot*. Cover and set aside. Soften the chopped onions in foaming butter over low heat, season and mix well then cook until golden, stirring frequently to prevent burning. Sprinkle with flour and stir it well into the butter. Add the hot water and beat well with a hand whisk to stop lumps forming. Simmer steadily for 30 minutes.

Meanwhile toast the bread lightly on both sides, halve the slices and place in a well-heated tureen, keep hot in a warm oven.

Pour the cream into a warm bowl, add a little soup, stir well, then return the mixture to the pan. Stir the soup well and pour it over the toasted bread. Leave in the oven for 5 minutes.

Serve in well-heated bowls with the *gringot* sprinkled thickly on top.

Note This soup is a meal in itself and needs only fresh fruit to follow.

Potage Crème de Poireaux à l'Ancienne
Old-fashioned Cream of Leek Soup

Serves 6

Eggs and cream are plentiful in Normandy where they serve this soup, making a humble dish into a highly nutritious meal.

6 large leeks, washed, trimmed and finely sliced, white and pale green leaves only
50g/2 oz butter
salt, white pepper

100g/4 oz stale light rye bread
1.2 litres/2¼ pints warm water
2 large egg yolks
150ml/¼ pint double cream

Soften the leeks in foaming butter in a large pan over medium heat. Add salt, cover, reduce the heat to low and simmer for 10 minutes without colouring, stirring occasionally.

Meanwhile soak the bread in cold water for a moment, and squeeze dry. Pour the warm water into the pan, crumble in the bread finely and season well. Stir and bring slowly to boiling point. Cover and simmer for 45 minutes, stirring occasionally.

Purée a couple of ladlefuls of soup in a blender or food processor, enough to thicken the soup a little, but bearing in mind the egg binding, which will thicken it further. Return the purée to the pan, bring the contents to boiling point and proceed to add the binding as for Soupe aux Coques on page 20. Serve immediately in heated soup plates, with croûtons handed separately.

Note This soup can be made more economically by substituting milk and butter for the egg and cream binding. Add 150ml/¼ pint milk to the soup when ready to serve, simmer until boiling again and beat in 25g/1 oz butter cut into small pieces.

Soupe aux Pois et au Lard
Pea Soup with Bacon

Serves 6

225g/8 oz split peas, soaked overnight in cold water
450g/1 lb leeks, washed, trimmed and thickly sliced, green included
225g/8 oz carrots, peeled and thinly sliced
1 lettuce, washed and finely shredded
450g/1 lb floury potatoes cut into large cubes
2 × 5ml spoons/2 teaspoons salt

3 litres/5 pints cold water
225g/8 oz lean streaky bacon in one piece, cut into fingers
white and black pepper
1 bouquet garni (see page 14)
6 thin slices stale rye or wholemeal bread
6 × 15ml spoons/6 tablespoons double cream (optional)

Drain the peas and boil in fresh water for 10 minutes. Put all the vegetables except the lettuce and potatoes into a large soup pan, add half the salt and cover with water. Add the bacon and bring slowly to boiling over medium heat. Skim off the froth as it rises. When clear, add pepper and the herbs. Reduce the heat and simmer for 1½ hours, until the peas are almost cooked. Add the lettuce and potatoes to the pan and simmer for a further 30 minutes, uncovered. Remove the herbs.

Cut the bread diagonally into half slices and place in the bottom of a tureen or large earthenware bowl. Pour the soup over them, cover and place in a moderate oven for 5 minutes to soak the bread. Serve a spoonful of cream stirred into each plateful of soup if desired.

HOT & COLD PÂTÉS, CROUSTADES & SALADS

The ingenuity displayed by French country people when it comes to not wasting anything edible is impressive.

On the farms of Vendée when a pig is slaughtered and the black puddings are made, even the water in which they were boiled is shared with appreciative neighbours. This same ingenuity is allowed free rein when it comes to making pâtés.

Hot savoury tarts known as *croustades* are a first-course speciality for Sunday lunch in France. They vary with the region, the family recipes and the season, and can either be made with pastry or with a bread base.

French country salads, like country appetites, are robust. Several of the recipes given in this chapter, although usually served as a first course, make an excellent salad lunch when served with crisp bread and a glass of wine.

Pâté D'Olives
Black Olive Pâté

Serves 4

Provençal country people, mainly fruit and vegetable farmers, have their own kinds of pâté made of olives, which are one of their important products. The traditional *tapenade* includes anchovies, but the less-known version, simply called pâté d'olives, depends solely on the quality of the fruit for its savour.

225g/8 oz black olives, crushed and stoned
1 small onion, finely chopped
1 small clove garlic, finely chopped
a pinch dried powdered thyme or rosemary,
  or 3 crushed juniper berries

black pepper
50g/2 oz butter, softened

Mash the olive flesh, onion and garlic to a fine paste in a mortar. Alternatively, blend smooth or pass twice through the fine grid of a mincer.
Add the herbs and season well.
Work in the softened butter to obtain a smooth cream. Check the seasoning and pack the mixture into an earthenware bowl. Cover and chill until required.
Serve with thin slices of light rye or wholemeal bread accompanied by a bottle of chilled Muscadet.

Notes Olives are more easily stoned if first lightly crushed with the end of a bottle.
It is essential for authentic flavour to buy the really black, rather small olives preserved in olive oil and not the large purple-black olives soaked in a vinegar solution, which many of our delicatessen shops now seem to favour.

Pâté de ma Grand-Mère
Hot Liver Pâté
Serves 4–5

Pâtés of a special kind served hot are a feature of country menus. This one is served as a main course.

100g/4 oz chicken livers, washed and trimmed
350g/12 oz pigs liver, washed and trimmed
1 clove garlic or 3 shallots, finely chopped
2 × 15ml spoons/2 tablespoons chopped parsley
3 medium sized eggs

25g/1 oz butter
25g/1 oz flour
600ml/1 pint milk
7.5ml/1½ teaspoons salt
2.5ml/½ teaspoon each black and white pepper, nutmeg
(a 1 litre/2 pint soufflé dish, thickly buttered)

Cut the livers into small pieces (remove parts stained yellow) and mix with garlic or shallots and parsley.

Put the mixture twice through the mincer or blend smooth. Beat the eggs in a mixing bowl and add the liver mixture.

Make a béchamel sauce with the butter, flour and milk (see page 10). Remove pan from the heat, beat in the liver mixture and season well.

Pour it into the buttered dish, cover with a piece of buttered greaseproof paper, then a piece of foil and tie them round. Make a small hole in the centre with a skewer. Cut a strip of foil 5cm/2 inches wide, wind it round a pencil to make a funnel and insert in the hole.

Stand the dish in a bain-marie and cook in the oven at 190°C/375°F/Gas 5 for 1¼ hours, replenishing the hot water if it evaporates.

The pâté is cooked when a metal skewer plunged down the funnel comes out clean. If not, cook for a further 15 minutes.

Leave to settle for a few minutes, then pass a thin-bladed knife dipped in hot water round the inside of the dish, place a heated serving plate on top, and quickly invert the pâté onto it.

Serve at once with Coulis de Tomates handed separately, see page 9.

Note What is left over can be pressed into a smaller dish just large enough to hold it and, when cold, covered with foil and chilled. Serve cut into slices with a green salad.

Pâté-Terrine de Campagne
Coarse Country Pâté

Serves 14–16

The very popular first course of pâté-en-terrine is mostly of the coarse kind on country tables. It can be cooked in a soufflé dish if there is no earthenware terrine to hand. It is an appetizing, if rather filling, start to a meal.

225g/8 oz chicken livers, washed and trimmed
175g/6 oz pigs liver, washed and trimmed
700g/1½ lb lean pork (leg or shoulder)
175g/6 oz pork fat or fat belly of pork, skinned and chopped
2 shallots, coarsely chopped
7.5ml/1½ teaspoons salt
2.5ml/½ teaspoon each black and white pepper, and grated nutmeg

2 × 15ml spoons/2 tablespoons brandy or dry vermouth
40g/1½ oz pistachio nuts, skinned and halved
225g/8 oz streaky bacon rashers
thick flour and water paste for sealing (optional)
(1.5 litre/3 pint terrine or soufflé dish, well buttered)

Prepare the livers as indicated on page 29.
Mince or blend them coarsely together with the pork, pork fat and shallots.
Add seasoning, brandy or vermouth and nuts and mix thoroughly.
Check seasoning.
Line the dish with rashers of bacon, leaving enough hanging over the sides to fold over. Fill with the prepared mixture and cover with ends of rashers.
If using a terrine, just cover the pâté with greaseproof paper and then the lid, sealed down with a roll of flour and water paste, wetting the edges of the dish and lid to make the paste stick.
If using a soufflé dish proceed as on page 29.
Place the dish in a bain-marie in the bottom half of the oven heated to 180°C/350°F/Gas 4 and cook for 20 minutes. Reduce the heat to 140°C/275°F/Gas 1 and cook for 2½ hours.
Test as advised on page 29.
When cooked, remove all covering except greaseproof paper, put a plate or piece of wood on top and a heavy weight on that to hold it down.
Leave to cool overnight before serving.

Note This pâté-en-terrine keeps very well when chilled or frozen.

Pâté-Terrine de Campagne

Pâté-Terrine de Poisson
Fish Pâté

This fish pâté served with a green salad makes an excellent summer lunch dish.

450g/1 lb huss or sole, boned and skinned
salt, black pepper, celery salt
4 × 15ml spoons/4 tablespoons lemon juice
   (not strained)
175g/6 oz butter, softened
peel of 1 large lemon, grated
100g/4 oz stale white breadcrumbs (must be
   oven baked)

350g/12 oz fresh haddock and brill, or
   whiting, finely chopped
3 × 15ml spoons/3 tablespoons chopped
   parsley
1 large egg, lightly beaten
3 × 15ml spoons/3 tablespoons milk
lemon slices for garnishing
(1 litre/2 pint soufflé dish, buttered)

Cut the huss or sole across into 1.5cm/½ inch wide strips. Arrange them in one layer on a large plate and season with salt and black pepper, sprinkle with half the lemon juice, scatter liberally with celery salt, mix well and cover.

To the butter add 5 ml/1 teaspoon salt, some pepper and the lemon peel. Add the breadcrumbs gradually, beating them in with a hand whisk.

Blend or mince finely the chopped fish, 30ml/2 tablespoons parsley and add remaining lemon juice. Mix this into the butter mixture thoroughly with a hand whisk. Beat the egg and milk with a pinch of salt and bind the fish mixture, or *farce*, with it.

Divide the filleted fish into two parts and the *farce* into three. Fill the dish first with a layer of *farce*, then a layer of fillets and so on ending with the *farce*. Press down firmly before covering.

Stand the dish in a bain-marie and cook in the lower half of the oven at 180°C/ 350°F/Gas 4 for 1½ hours. When cooked, turn off the heat and leave the dish inside with the door ajar until quite cold. Do not remove the coverings until ready to serve.

Unmould as advised on page 29. Cut half into 5mm/¼ inch slices, arrange on a serving plate and garnish with lemon slices and remaining parsley.

Return the remainder to the dish, cover and chill for further use.

Pâte Brisée
Shortcrust Pastry

Serves 4–6

This method produces perfect pastry for *croustades* or any other tarts with a moist filling.

175g/6 oz plain flour
salt
75g/3 oz butter, softened to a cream
1 medium sized egg yolk, beaten

1 × 15ml spoon/1 tablespoon cold water
(a 20cm/8 inch flan tin with loose base, buttered)

Sift the flour and a pinch of salt into a mixing bowl to make a mound. Make a well in the centre and drop in the butter, yolk, another pinch of salt and the water.

Mix these last three ingredients together with a fork, holding the bowl with the other hand. Then, turning the bowl meanwhile, gather in the flour with the fingers, adding a few drops of water if necessary, to make a soft ball. Wrap in greaseproof paper and chill for 30 minutes.

Roll out the pastry thickly, fold into four and roll again. Fold a second time and chill for 30 minutes before use.

Note To serve 6–8 use 225g/8 oz flour, 100g/4 oz butter, 1 large egg yolk and 1.5 × 15ml spoons/1½ tablespoons cold water. This quantity of pastry will line a 25cm/10 inch flan tin with a loose base.

For even larger numbers use the above quantities and increase the fillings by half.

Variation

For *pâte sucrée* used with fruit or other sweet tarts, use these same ingredients, but omit the salt except for a pinch in the beaten egg, and add 1.5 × 15ml spoons/1½ tablespoons caster sugar to the flour for the smaller quantity, and 2 × 15ml spoons/2 tablespoons for the larger.

The correct consistency for *pâte sucrée* is obtained by *foulage* – push the pastry ball along the board firmly with the heel of the hand. Reform the ball with the fingers, and repeat 4 or 5 times. Cut it into quarters, put one on top of the other, press down lightly and repeat 3 or 4 times.

Croûtes au Kirsch
Kirsch and Ham Rarebit

Serves 6

In winter time the mountain farms produce snacks˙ that send up the body temperature in a trice—none more quickly than this rarebit.

3 × 15ml spoons/3 tablespoons double cream
225g/8 oz Gruyère cheese, grated
7 large eggs
pepper, nutmeg
100g/4 oz butter
4 × 15ml spoons/4 tablespoons oil

6 slices bread (cut 2cm/³/₄ inch thick), crusts removed
1 × 5ml spoon/1 teaspoon vinegar
6 × 15ml spoons/6 tablespoons kirsch
6 thin slices boiled ham, fat removed

Beat the cream, grated cheese and 1 egg together, season with pepper and nutmeg and set aside.

Melt 25g/1 oz butter with 15ml/1 tablespoon oil in a large frying pan and when foaming colour the bread golden on both sides, adding more butter and oil as required.

Meanwhile poach the remaining 6 eggs very lightly in a large panful of salted water with the vinegar.

As the bread colours, take each slice out of the pan, place it in a small flameproof dish, sprinkle with kirsch and cover with a slice of ham. Drain the eggs well and place them on top. Beat the cheese mixture again and pour it over the eggs.

Have the grill heated to maximum and place the croûtes under it. Leave just long enough for the cheese to melt.

Serve without delay with a liqueur glass of kirsch for each person.

Croûtes au Kirsch

La Fouace aux Herbes
Curd Cheese and Herb Tart
Serves 4 as a main course, 6 as a first course

Rabelais is known to have relished a *fouace*, the savoury tart made with curd cheese in the farmhouses of the Deux-Sèvres. The rounded dark brown surface of the *fouace* is distinctive on country market stalls where it is still sold.

pâté brisée for 4–6 (see page 33)
3 medium sized eggs, separated
salt, black pepper
25g/1 oz butter
2 bunches spring onions trimmed and
  chopped, green included
8 large sorrel leaves or 1 × 15ml spoon/1
  tablespoon chopped tarragon

2 × 15ml spoons/2 tablespoons chopped
  parsley
2 × 15ml spoons/2 tablespoons chopped
  chives
150g/5 oz curd cheese
1 × 15ml spoon/1 tablespoon milk (optional)
(a 20cm/8 inch flan tin with loose base,
  buttered)

Remove the pastry from the refrigerator 15 minutes before use.
Roll out the pastry, line and trim the tin. Do not chill. Heat the oven to 190°C/375°F/Gas 5. Cover a baking sheet with foil and place in oven. Beat the egg whites to a stiff peak with a pinch of salt and chill.
Melt the butter in a frying pan, and, when foaming, add the onions and cook slowly until soft. Add the sorrel cut into strips (if used) and stir until wilted. Add the herbs, season well and mix, adding more butter if the mixture seems dry. Leave to cool. Spread over the bottom of the pastry case.
Beat the egg yolks into the curd cheese and season highly. If the mixture is stiff add milk, then beat until it is the consistency of thick cream. Beat the egg whites again until very stiff and *fold* into the cheese mixture. *Do not beat or stir.* Pour into the pastry case and bake for 35 minutes until well risen and dark brown on top.
Allow to cool a little, remove rim of flan tin and serve warm or cold with a green salad.

Salade de Betteraves à Cru
Raw Beetroot Salad

Serves 6 as a first course

---

3 × 5ml spoons/3 teaspoons tarragon-
flavoured wine vinegar
150ml/¼ pint double cream
salt, black pepper

1 × 15ml spoon/1 tablespoon finely chopped
tarragon
350g/12 oz raw beetroot, peeled and grated

Mix the vinegar into the cream, season and stir in the tarragon. Check seasoning and add a few more drops of vinegar if necessary. Pour over the beetroot. Mix well and allow to stand for 1 hour before serving.

Salade de Pommes de Terre Chaude
Hot Potato and Sausage Salad

Serves 4 as a lunch or supper dish, 6 as a first course

1.2kg/2½ lb red-skinned potatoes, scrubbed
only
225g/8 oz smoked sausage, thickly sliced
1 × 15ml spoon/1 tablespoon corn oil
150ml/¼ pint dry white wine

salt, black pepper
6 × 15ml spoons/6 tablespoons vinaigrette
(see page 13)
2 × 15ml spoons/2 tablespoons chopped
chives

Boil the potatoes slowly until just tender—do not overcook. Leave until cool enough to handle.
Sauté the sausage in hot oil until golden. Drain on absorbent paper and keep hot.
Pour the wine into a large heated bowl. Peel the potatoes, put them straight in the bowl and turn in the wine. Then cut into thick slices, return them to the bowl, season well and pour the vinaigrette over them. Turn the slices over to coat with dressing, cover, and place over a pan of simmering water.
Add the chives to the sausage rings and mix them lightly into the potatoes. Check seasoning. Serve hot with the same wine as that used in the recipe.

Céleri en Salade
Celery and Cheese Salad

Serves 4 as a lunch dish, 6 as a first course

2 heads of celery, washed, dried and cut
    small, green leaves included
salt, black pepper
100g/4 oz walnut halves

100g/4 oz Roquefort or Stilton cheese
1 × 15ml spoon/1 tablespoon brandy
4 × 15ml spoons/4 tablespoons vinaigrette
    (see page 13)

Place celery in a salad bowl, season, add nuts and chill until required.
Crumble the cheese into a small bowl, crush with a fork and work in the
brandy until the cheese is soft. Now mix in the vinaigrette little by little,
beating constantly until thoroughly blended.
To serve, pour the dressing over the celery and nuts, mix well and serve
immediately.

Salade de Haricots Verts aux Echalotes
Green Bean and Shallot Salad

Serves 4

450g/1 lb small green beans, topped, tailed
    and left whole
salt, black pepper
2–3 5ml spoons/2–3 teaspoons lemon juice

3 × 15ml spoons/3 tablespoons double cream
1 × 15ml spoon/1 tablespoon chopped chervil
    or parsley
1 shallot, peeled and finely chopped

Cook the beans in boiling salted water until only just tender. They must
remain slightly crisp.
Meanwhile beat 10ml/2 teaspoons lemon juice into the cream, season well
and stir in the chervil or parsley and shallot.
Drain the beans thoroughly and add hot to the dressing. Turn them over
carefully to coat well. Check seasoning and serve lightly chilled.
This salad made with *mange tout* peas instead of green beans is excellent.

The Bean and Shallot Salad can also be made with mange tout *peas*

EGGS, RICE & PASTA

Eggs are the perennial stand-by in the world's kitchens but the French farmer's wife can show the rest of us several tricks when it comes to making them into an unusual and interesting dish.

Rice she treats too in many ways, serving it plain or savoury with certain meat dishes instead of potatoes, but always dry and fluffy, or she may include it among the ingredients of a substantial salad.

Rice and pasta, whether in the form of spaghetti, macaroni or tagliatelli (flat noodles) are not the prerogative of the Italians. They are now part of the Frenchman's staple diet, although they were originally introduced by the Romans. In Provençal dialect noodles are known as *li taiarin* and are usually made at home. But their international popularity has made it possible to buy them, made fresh daily, from most Italian delicatessen shops.

Riz au Blanc
Boiled Rice

Serves 4

1 × 5ml spoon/1 teaspoon salt
1 thick slice of lemon
225g/8 oz long-grain rice

25g/1 oz butter or 2 tablespoons olive oil
black pepper

Rub the inside rim of a very large pan with buttered paper to prevent boiling over and fill three-quarters full with boiling water. Add salt and lemon and when boiling scatter the rice over the surface gradually. Cook for exactly 10 minutes, then test. Cook for a few minutes more if necessary.
Meanwhile heat the oven to 170°C/325°F/Gas 3. Put the butter or oil in a large shallow dish and place dish in oven. Tip the rice into a colander and hold under cold running water for 3 or 4 minutes, turning occasionally.
Empty the rice into the buttered dish, season well and spread out with a fork. Place in the lower half of the oven to dry slowly. Turn it over occasionally and spread it out again. When rice is hot, dry and fluffy, serve immediately.

Boules de Riz
Stuffed Rice Balls

Serves 4

Farmhouse larders are famous for the amount of leftovers they can collect, probably because such vast amounts of food are prepared in the first place. But Frenchwomen have a genius for using leftovers. In fact, a double quantity of rice is often prepared deliberately so that Boules de Riz can be made another day.

2 medium sized eggs, beaten
325g/11 oz cold cooked seasoned rice
salt, black pepper
150g/5 oz Gruyère cheese, cut in one slice 1
  cm/½ inch thick, then into cubes

6–7 × 15ml spoons/6–7 tablespoons fine dry
  breadcrumbs
oil for deep frying

Mix the eggs and rice carefully and season well. Scoop up 15ml/1 tablespoonful, push a cube of cheese into the centre and place another tablespoon of rice on top. Shape into a ball between two spoons or wetted palms. Roll in crumbs and place on greaseproof paper. Chill for 30 minutes.
Heat the oil to 190°C/375°F.
Line a baking sheet with absorbent paper and place it in the oven at low temperature. Fry the balls 4 at a time for about 5 minutes in the heated oil until golden brown. Drain on the paper in the oven and serve very hot with a green salad.

Note This dish can be kept hot for 10 minutes if left in the oven.

Li Taiarin à la Crème
Noodles with Cream and Cheese

Serves 4 as a main course,
6 as a first course

4 × 15ml spoons/4 tablespoons double cream
100g/4 oz butter, softened to a cream
100g/4 oz Parmesan cheese

1 potato, very finely sliced
450g/1 lb fresh noodles
salt, black pepper

Work the cream into the butter until smooth, then add the cheese gradually until well incorporated.

Butter the rim of a large pan to prevent boiling over, fill it nearly full with boiling water, add the potato slices, place over medium-high heat and when boiling fast, drop in the noodles. Stir to prevent sticking and boil for exactly 7 minutes.

Test; they should be slightly firm when bitten into, not soft. Drain well, empty into a hot bowl and season generously. Pour the cream mixture on top, turning the mass over and over quickly with a spoon and fork until well coated.

Serve immediately on hot plates.

Notes Sliced potato helps the noodles to absorb cheese or other sauce.

For plain buttered noodles served with meat or game, cut 50g/2 oz butter into small cubes. Drop them into a heated serving bowl and pour the drained noodles over them. Season well, mix thoroughly and serve immediately.

In Provence, one of the most popular ways of
serving noodles (called li taiarin) *is with*
Pestou (page 12)

Li Taiarin au Jambon
Noodles with Ham, Chicken and Cheese

Serves 4 as a main course, 6 as a first course

100g/4 oz button mushrooms, wiped, trimmed and finely sliced
2 × 15ml spoons/2 tablespoons lemon juice
450g/1 lb fresh noodles
1 potato, finely sliced
salt, black pepper
50g/2 oz butter

1 × 15ml spoon/1 tablespoon flour
450ml/¾ pint milk
100g/4 oz lean boiled ham, finely slivered, fat removed
100g/4 oz cold chicken, finely slivered
75g/3 oz Gruyère cheese, grated

Turn the mushrooms in lemon juice to prevent discoloration. Cook the noodles with the potatoes in salted water as described on page 42, but keep them under-cooked. Drain well and keep hot in a colander over boiling water.

Melt half the butter in a large pan and make a béchamel sauce adding flour and milk as described on page 10.

Melt the remaining butter and keep warm.

Add the mushroom slices, ham and chicken to the sauce, season and cook together for 3–4 minutes, stirring constantly. Add the noodles, stir thoroughly to incorporate and add half the cheese; draw the pan from the heat and stir until it has melted. Check seasoning.

Pour into a gratin dish, pour the melted butter over the top, scatter with the remaining cheese and place under a very hot grill for 4–5 minutes until lightly coloured.

Serve without delay.

Variation
Plain noodles can be served with Pestou (see page 12).

Oeufs en Surtout
Eggs with Anchovies and Capers

Serves 4

The French, according to Thomas Moore, had in the eighteenth century already found 686 ways to dress eggs, and this he found endearing. He did not however mention the country people's gift for naming them.

What could be more apt than Eggs in Overcoats to describe soft-baked eggs covered by a thick mousse flavoured with anchovies and capers.

2 × 5ml spoons/2 teaspoons capers, drained and coarsely chopped
6 anchovy fillets
2 × 15ml spoons/2 tablespoons chopped chives or spring onions
2 × 15ml spoons/2 tablespoons chopped parsley

6 large eggs, 2 only separated
salt, black pepper, grated nutmeg
(4 shallow saucer-sized ovenproof dishes, buttered

Heat the oven to 180°C/350°C/Gas 4 and place a baking sheet and the 4 dishes on the middle shelf.

Chop the capers, anchovies, chives or spring onions and parsley finely together. Mix this with 2 egg yolks. Season lightly with salt and generously with pepper and nutmeg. Beat well.

Beat the 2 whites to a soft peak and chill. Break the remaining eggs into wetted saucers, slide 1 egg into each dish and season the yolks. *Fold* the egg whites into the anchovy mixture and quickly divide it between the 4 dishes to cover the eggs and touch the sides of the dish. Bake for exactly 10 minutes, no more, and serve without delay.

Omelette au Thon Marine
Tuna Omelet

Serves 4 as a main course, 6 as a first course

2 × 5ml spoons/2 teaspoons butter, softened
1 × 5ml spoon/1 teaspoon finely chopped
  parsley
4 soft herring roes
salt, black pepper

½ clove garlic, crushed
40g/1½ oz butter, cut into small pieces
50g/2 oz canned tuna, drained and shredded
6 large eggs
juice of ½ lemon

Work the softened butter into the parsley. Chill, and when firm, cut into small pieces.

Blanch the roes in boiling salted water for 3 minutes. Drain well. Put the roes, garlic, 25g/1 oz butter and tuna into a saucepan, place over low heat and mix well. Break the eggs into a bowl, season and mix well with a fork. As soon as the butter in the pan melts, pour the tuna mixture into the eggs and stir thoroughly.

Heat a large frying pan over medium heat, dry, for a few moments. Add remaining butter and when foaming, coat the pan. Pour in the egg mixture. Draw it in from the sides to the centre with a spatula to allow the liquid to run out and loosen the edges as they set.

While the omelet is still liquid on the surface, fold it over and slide it onto a heated serving dish in which half the pieces of parsley butter have been placed. Dot with the remaining parsley butter, sprinkle with lemon juice and serve immediately.

Note To crush garlic easily without a press chop it first, sprinkle with salt and crush it with the flat of a knife blade or the bottom of a bottle.

FISH

The extensive coasts of France produce fish of infinite variety. Even the smallest towns, in their covered food halls and weekly street markets, offer an average of 30 varieties of freshly caught salt-water and fresh-water fish in all but the most rigorous seasons. The variety of shellfish is also considerable. In consequence the French repertory of fish recipes is extensive.

The recipes given here can be adapted to any of the fish found in more limited variety in our markets.

Truites à la Bretonne
Trout with Shrimps and Potatoes

Serves 4

5 × 15ml spoons/5 tablespoons corn oil	*seasoned flour*
450g/1 lb potatoes, cut into cubes	*50g/2 oz butter*
4 trout, approx. 225g/8 oz each, gutted, washed and dried, fins removed, head left on	*2 tablespoons capers*
	175g/6 oz peeled shrimps
	2 × 15ml spoons/2 tablespoons chopped parsley
salt, black pepper	

Heat 45ml/3 tablespoons oil in a *sauteuse* or large frying pan over medium heat and cook the potatoes until crisp and golden. Keep hot.

Dip the trout in seasoned flour and shake off excess.

Heat remaining oil in another pan and cook the trout for 15–20 minutes, turning them over when one side is golden brown.

Drain the fish, arrange in a heated serving dish, cover and keep hot.

Wipe out the potato pan with absorbent paper, replace over moderately high heat and melt the butter until foaming. Add potatoes and when crisp add capers, shrimps and seasoning and mix well. Shake the pan to prevent sticking. Pour this mixture around the trout and sprinkle with parsley.

Note Do not *cook* the shrimps or they will toughen. Just heat them through.

Matelote D'Anguilles à la Bourgeoise
Mixed Fish in White Wine Sauce

Serves 6

A good *matelote*, or fish stew, is a favourite with fisherman since it can be used to include their whole catch of fresh-water fish: eels, carp, huss, pike and even very small fish.

1.5–2kg/3–4 lb huss, eel, carp or any firm-fleshed fish, cleaned, washed and dried
55g/2¼ oz butter
12 small onions, pickling size
6 shallots, finely chopped
1 bay leaf
1 sprig fennel

750ml/1¼ pints dry white wine
salt, black pepper
225g/8 oz button mushrooms, wiped, dried and sliced
1 × 5ml spoon/1 teaspoon flour
2 medium sized egg yolks, beaten
5 × 15ml spoons/5 tablespoons double cream

Cut the fish into serving pieces. Leave any small ones whole.

Melt 50g/2 oz butter in a *sauteuse* or large frying pan over medium heat and, when foaming, add the onions and shallots. Stir well to coat with butter, add the fish and turn it over. Add herbs, wine and seasoning.

Reduce heat to low and bring slowly to boiling. Ignite the wine and baste the ingredients until the flames die.

Add the mushrooms to the pan and cook very gently for 10–15 minutes so that the fish does not disintegrate.

When tender, remove the fish and onions with a slotted spoon to a heated serving dish, cover and keep hot. Leave the pan over low heat to reduce the liquids a little.

Make a *beurre manié* by working the remaining butter into the flour with a knife blade until smooth. Drop this into the pan and stir until incorporated.

Remove the herbs and beat the sauce well with a hand whisk.

Increase the heat a little and simmer faster for 3–4 minutes. Remove from heat, beat the egg yolks into the cream and add to the sauce. Stir over minimum heat until thickened.

Pour over fish and serve immediately with boiled new potatoes.

Poisson en Daube
Braised Fish with Herbs

Serves 4–6

The French country recipe for cooking large fish, either whole or in big pieces, is very suitable for the extra large herring and mackerel we find in certain seasons in our own markets. Grey mullet too, or any large firm-fleshed fish, is delicious cooked with vegetables in this old-fashioned way.

225g/8 oz each carrots, white of leek, and onion, peeled, cleaned and chopped
25g/1 oz each chives and parsley, washed, dried and chopped
100g/4 oz sorrel (optional) washed, dried and chopped
salt, black pepper
2 × 15ml spoons/2 tablespoons olive or corn oil

1 large fish (about 1–1.5kg/2–3 lb)
peel of 2 small oranges, cut into pieces
1 bouquet garni (see page 14)
150ml/¼ pint dry white wine
4 × 15ml spoons/4 tablespoons brandy or dry vermouth

Mix the vegetables and fresh herbs and season well.

Pour the oil into a *cocotte*, spread half the vegetables in the bottom, place the fish on top, season well and cover with the remaining vegetables and the orange peel. Add the bouquet garni, wine and brandy or vermouth. Cover with a tightly fitting lid and cook over minimum heat until the fish is tender when pierced with a skewer (about 1 hour, depending on the thickness of the fish).

To serve, remove the bouquet garni, and orange peel, arrange the fish in a heated dish and pour the vegetables and juices around it.

Note If an earthenware casserole is used, bake in the oven at 170°C/325°F/Gas 3 for about 1½ hours.

If the pan lid does not fit tightly, put a piece of foil over the rim and force the lid down over it.

Cabillaud à la Provençale
Cod with Tomato and Herb Sauce

Serves 6

2 × 15ml spoons/2 tablespoons olive oil
4 shallots, chopped
225g/8 oz canned tomatoes, drained and
  chopped
salt, black pepper
1 × 5ml spoon/1 teaspoon herbes du Midi (see
  page 16) or mixed dried thyme,

rosemary, basil, fennel
6 thick slices cod, hake, bass or other large
  firm-fleshed fish, washed and dried
flour for coating
50g/2 oz butter
2 × 15ml spoons/2 tablespoons corn oil

Heat the olive oil in a small pan, add the shallots, tomatoes, salt, pepper and herbs. Cook over brisk heat, stirring until the moisture has evaporated and the mixture is soft and thick. Reduce heat to low and keep hot.

Season the fish on both sides and dip in flour. Heat the butter with the corn oil in a large frying pan until foaming and cook the fish until golden, 4–5 minutes on each side.

Arrange on a heated serving dish, pour the reduced tomato sauce over the fish and serve immediately.

Note The juice drained from the tomatoes can be added to vegetable soup.

Raie aux Câpres
Skate with Caper Sauce

Serves 4

Nouvelle cuisine uses first-quality ingredients in the simplest way, to produce delicious results. In many cases the dishes resemble old country recipes like the one given below.

4 pieces skate, about 225g/8 oz each, scrubbed and washed
1 large onion, quartered
1 litre/1¼ pints water

3 × 15ml spoons/3 tablespoons tarragon vinegar
1 bouquet garni (see page 14)
salt, black pepper
Sauce aux Câpres (see page 10)

Put the fish in a large pan and add the onion, water, vinegar, herbs and seasoning.
Place over low heat. Bring very slowly to boiling point, then poach gently for 10–15 minutes, depending on the thickness of the fish. Watch it carefully because skate can easily fall apart. When tender, drain well and place the fish on a heated serving dish.
Pour the sauce over the fish and serve immediately.

Variation

For more impressive presentation carefully drain and dry the fish on absorbent paper while it is still slightly undercooked, then sauté in 50g/2 oz butter, brought to foaming in a large frying pan. When golden on one side turn the fish over and add 15ml/1 tablespoon wine vinegar and the same measure of chopped capers to the butter. Mix well, season and serve with this sauce only.

Gratin de Sole à la Gironde
Baked Sole with Fresh Herbs

Serves 6

25g/1 oz butter
15g/½ oz flour
2 shallots, finely chopped
175g/6 oz mushrooms, peeled and chopped
2 × 15ml spoons/2 tablespoons chopped
parsley
1 × 15ml spoon/1 tablespoon chopped chives

salt, black pepper
5 × 15ml spoons/5 tablespoons stale white
breadcrumbs
6 fillets of sole or brill, washed and dried
150ml/¼ pint dry white wine
150ml/¼ pint bouillon
50g/2 oz Gruyère cheese, grated

Butter a large gratin dish with half the butter. Sprinkle thickly with flour and shake out the excess.

Mix the shallots, mushrooms, parsley and chives together and season.

Heat the remaining butter in a frying pan and, when foaming, fry 45ml/3 tablespoons breadcrumbs until pale golden. Drain on absorbent paper.

Sprinkle remaining breadcrumbs in the prepared dish and cover with half the vegetable mixture. Cover with the fish, placing the fillets head to tail. Cover with the rest of the vegetables. Season lightly. Mix the wine and bouillon and pour down the sides of the dish. Toss the buttered crumbs and grated cheese together and sprinkle evenly over the contents.

Bake for 25–35 minutes at 180°C/350°F/Gas 4 until the gratin is browned, and the liquid bubbling.

Serve immediately with small new potatoes.

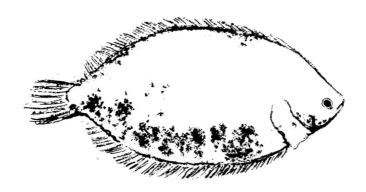

Pain de Thon
Tuna Mould

Serves 6

450g/1 lb fillets of whiting, washed and dried
1 lemon, peel and pith removed, flesh sliced
1 bouquet garni
salt, black pepper
300g/10 oz canned tuna, drained and
    shredded
2 × 15ml/2 tablespoons stale breadcrumbs
4 × 15ml/4 tablespoons olive oil
2.5ml/½ teaspoon paprika

3 large eggs, beaten
2 × 15ml/2 tablespoons chopped parsley
2 × 15ml/2 tablespoons chopped chives
2 × 15ml/2 tablespoons chopped chervil
    (optional)
2 × 5ml/2 teaspoons concentrated tomato
    purée
herb mayonnaise (see page 11)
parsley sprigs

Place the whiting in one layer in a *sauteuse* or a large frying pan, cover barely with water and add all the lemon slices but 2. Add bouquet garni and seasoning and bring slowly to boiling over low heat. Simmer for 5 minutes, then drain.

Shred the whiting and mix with the tuna, breadcrumbs, oil, seasoning and paprika. Mix well and pass the mixture through a mouli-légumes (coarse grid), or a mincer. Check for seasoning and add lemon juice to taste from reserved slices.

Beat the eggs and fresh herbs together, season and work into the fish.

Line a cake tin with well-buttered foil and fill with the mixture. Cook in a bain-marie in the oven at 190°C/375°F/Gas 5, for about 50 minutes.

When firm in the centre, leave until cold and chill overnight.

An hour before serving beat the tomato purée into the mayonnaise. Transfer to a sauceboat and chill.

Unmould the fish onto a serving dish and garnish with parsley sprigs. Serve the mayonnaise separately.

Pain de Thon with Herb Mayonnaise (page 11)

PORK, BEEF, VEAL & LAMB

French methods of cooking meat are individual.

Instead of roasting a joint with fat in an open roasting tin and basting the contents frequently the French housewife cooks it in a closed vessel and does not baste it at all.

Dufeu is the trade name of the heavy iron casserole which she uses. It has a sunken lid which is filled with water, thus creating condensation which prevents the meat from drying and reduces shrinkage to a minimum. In this way joints of beef, veal and lamb are cooked to perfection and served tender, juicy, and pink inside as they should be. Pork is perhaps the most popular meat in country households and has been since the days of Ancient Gaul. It was the Roman conquerors who introduced their method of dry pickling with salt, and pork proved to be the ideal meat for this process. This way of pickling is still used today, notably for making pickled belly pork. This is used in many country dishes, either cut into *lardons*, the short thick strips used to flavour vegetable recipes, casseroles and omelets, or cooked in one piece in soup to which it gives its flavour and is then served with vegetables as the main course.

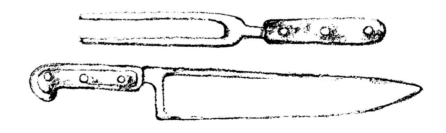

Petit Salé
Dry-Cured Pickled Pork

1.5kg/3 lb fat belly of pork
3× 5ml spoons/3 teaspoons saltpetre

salt, black pepper

Cut the pork into 3 oblong pieces, and remove the rind from the one reserved for lardons by placing it rind-side down, and with a very sharp knife pressing down on the rind while cutting and rolling back the meat at the same time. Jab the three pieces on both sides with a pointed knife, piercing right through. Sprinkle each side in turn evenly with 2.5ml/½ teaspoon saltpetre, rub it in with the palm of the hand, sprinkle with salt, rub this in, and then sprinkle again with the salt and coarsely ground black pepper, treating the entire surface of the meat. Place in an earthenware dish and cover with a colander. Leave in a cool airy larder.

Turn the meat after 3 days. Turn again after another 3 days and if the surface is dry, sprinkle with a little more salt. Leave for a further 3 days. Brush off excess salt, wipe with a dry cloth, wrap in waxed paper or foil and chill. The piece reserved for lardons should be rolled tightly before wrapping.

Prior to cooking, pickled pork must be well washed under cold running water, then blanched, i.e. placed in a pan of boiling water, boiled for 5 minutes, drained and dried.

To make lardons, cut the reserved slice into thumb-sized strips 1cm/½ inch thick, blanch and use as directed, but salt the dish very *lightly* until seasoning is checked during cooking.

To store a larger quantity of pickled pork, scald an earthenware crock with boiling water, dry thoroughly and rub with salt, place the pork in it, layering the pieces with sprinklings of coarse sea salt, a sprig of thyme, a bay leaf, some black peppercorns and cloves in between each layer. Cover the crock with muslin and store in a cool airy place.

Note Saltpetre is available from chemists' shops.

Poireaux à la Fermière
Pork and Leeks in Red Wine

Serves 6 as a main course

Making the most of good simple ingredients is one of the gifts of the country cook. This is the dish with which she regales the farm workers when the leek crop is in full season.

750g/1½ lb lean pickled belly of pork (see page 57) cut into 6 thick slices
20 small leeks, cleaned and trimmed, dark green left on
white pepper, cayenne, ground cloves
600ml/1 pint red wine
200ml/⅓ pint water

12 thick slices smoked sausage
15g/½ oz butter
2 × 15ml spoons/2 tablespoons breadcrumbs
2 × 15ml spoons/2 tablespoons parsley, chopped
1 large egg yolk, beaten

Blanch the pork for 5 minutes.
Drain well and arrange in one layer in a *sauteuse*. Put the leeks on top head to tail, sprinkle with pepper, cayenne and a generous pinch of cloves, no salt. Pour the wine and water, mixed, down the sides of the dish. Cover with a sheet of buttered greaseproof paper and force the lid down over it to seal.
Simmer over minimum heat for 1½ hours without removing the lid.
Sauté the sausage slices in butter, then dip them into the breadcrumbs and parsley mixed together. Heat the oven to 190°C/375°F/Gas 5.
When the leeks and pork are cooked, move from the casserole without disturbing the layers and arrange in a gratin dish. Pour the liquid into a bowl and skim off all fat.
Beat the egg yolk in a bowl with 175ml/6 fl oz of the liquid, beating it in gradually with a hand whisk. Check seasoning and pour this binding over the leeks. Garnish with cooked sausage slices, scatter the rest of the breadcrumbs and parsley over them and bake for 20–30 minutes until well browned on top.
Serve with thin slices of rye or wholemeal bread.

Poireaux à la Fermière

Croquettes de Porc
Pork Croquettes

Serves 4

This delicious pork dish is a great favourite for family reunions because it can be prepared beforehand and then takes only a short time to cook and serve.

40g/1½ oz butter
3 large shallots, finely chopped
75g/3 oz stale breadcrumbs, soaked in 150ml/
  ¼ pint milk
450g/1lb sparerib of pork, rind and bone
  removed, coarsely minced
salt, white pepper and grated nutmeg
250ml/8 fl oz dry white wine
2 medium sized eggs, separated

1 × 15ml spoon/1 tablespoon olive or corn oil
12 small onions, pickling size
seasoned flour
1 clove garlic
1 bouquet garni (see page 14)
150ml/¼ pint bouillon (see page 18)
12 small potatoes
2 × 15ml spoons/2 tablespoons boiling water
1 × 15ml spoon/1 tablespoon chopped parsley

Heat a third of the butter in a frying pan over low heat. Cook the shallots until soft. Squeeze all the moisture from the breadcrumbs and crumble into a large bowl, adding shallots, pan juices, pork, seasoning and nutmeg. Stir in 75ml/5 tablespoons wine and the egg yolks one at a time. Mix well and check seasoning.

Heat the remaining butter and the oil in a *sauteuse* or very large frying pan over medium heat and brown the onions on one side.

Beat the whites to a very stiff peak and *fold* into the pork mixture. Roll one heaped tablespoonful in seasoned flour. Turn the onions over, and place each ball of meat in the pan as rolled. Arrange in one layer and colour on all sides, shaking the pan to prevent sticking.

When crusted add garlic, bouquet garni and the remaining wine and bouillon mixed, poured down the sides of the pan. Add the potatoes, reduce heat and bring slowly to boiling point. Season, cover and cook for 30 minutes until potatoes are tender.

To serve transfer croquettes, potatoes and onions to a heated serving dish and keep hot. Remove bouquet garni from the pan, pour in the boiling water, scrape the base well to incorporate meat juices and pour over the meat and vegetables. Garnish with parsley and serve immediately.

Note For 6–8 people, double the quantities given and cook in a heavy roasting tin covered with foil, on top of the cooker.

Beekenofe Alsacien
Alsatian Hotpot

Serves 4

1kg/2lb potatoes, thickly sliced
225g/8 oz onions, finely sliced
225g/8 oz young carrots, peeled and finely
    sliced
350g/12 oz boned blade of pork, cut into
    5cm/2 inch pieces

225g/8 oz shoulder of lamb, cut as above
225g/8 oz shoulder of veal, cut as above
salt and black pepper
about 400ml/³⁄₄ pint Riesling or other dry
    white wine
25g/1oz butter

Butter a large earthenware casserole and fill it in layers with seasoned pototoes, onions and carrots then some of the meats mixed, until the dish is full, ending with potatoes in overlapping rows.
Pour the wine down the sides of the dish to barely cover, dot with butter and cover with buttered foil and the lid.
Bake for 2 hours in the centre of the oven at 180°C/350°F/Gas 4.
Remove the coverings and let the potatoes brown until crisp.
Serve immediately in the dish.

Ragoût de Porc
Ragoût of Pork with Tomatoes

Serves 6

1.5–2kg/3–4 lb thick end of belly pork, rind
    removed and bones chined
1 × 15ml spoon/1 tablespoon flour
600g/1¼ lb large tomatoes, washed and dried

3 medium-large onions, halved
1 bouquet garni (see page 14)
salt, white and black pepper
12 small potatoes

Cut the thick meaty end of pork into serving portions. Divide the bones and their meat into 6 pieces.
Put the latter into a large frying pan over low heat to render their fat. When well coloured, remove, drain on absorbent paper and place in a *cocotte*. In the fat in the pan colour the remaining meat, drain and add to the *cocotte*. Sprinkle with flour and stir to coat the ingredients. Add tomatoes, onions, herbs and seasoning. Add enough warm water to barely cover, increase heat to medium and when boiling reduce to low, cover and simmer for 1½ hours. At this point place the potatoes on the surface of the ragoût, cover and simmer for 30 minutes. Remove the bouquet garni and serve immediately.

Émincés de Boeuf
Steak in Mustard and Cream Sauce

Serves 6

This dish of tender steak in a mustard and cream sauce is ideal for entertaining, because it requires little preparation and is cooked in very few minutes.

60g/2½ oz butter
6 medium thin slices of rump steak, fat removed, cut into strips 1cm/½ inch × 5cm/2 inches
4 shallots, finely chopped
300ml/½ pint double cream

1 × 5ml spoon/1 teaspoon strong French mustard
salt, black pepper
1 × 5ml spoon/1 teaspoon potato flour or cornflour (optional)
1 × 5ml spoon/1 teaspoon water (optional)

Heat half the butter in a frying pan over medium heat. When foaming, add half the meat, turning the strips to seal on both sides. They must remain rare. Remove from the pan. Keep hot, seal the rest and put all the meat and pan juices together.

In the remaining butter cook the shallots until soft. Stir in half the cream and scrape up the meat residue. Increase the heat slightly and stir until the cream is thickened and lightly coloured. Stir in the remaining cream, reduce the heat and *gradually* stir in the mustard. Season and stir in the meat and juices. Heat but do not boil. Serve without delay with Riz au Blanc (see page 40) or buttered noodles.

Note If the sauce is too liquid before adding the mustard, bind it with the potato flour and water mixed. Replace the pan over low heat, bring to the first bubble, add the meat and juices, reheat and add the mustard when the pan is removed from the heat.

Émincés de Boeuf with buttered noodles

Bœuf Batellerie
Beef in Red Wine and Anchovy Sauce

Serves 4

700g/1½ lb chuck steak in 1 large slice 2.5cm/
  1 inch thick
8 black peppercorns, crushed, salt
1 × 5ml spoon/1 teaspoon dried thyme
2 cloves garlic, unpeeled and halved
3 × 15ml spoons/3 tablespoons chopped
  parsley
2 carrots, peeled and sliced
2 onions, sliced
2 shallots, finely sliced
3 × 15ml spoons/3 tablespoons red wine
  vinegar

4 × 15ml spoons/4 tablespoons olive oil
150ml/¼ pint red wine
SAUCE
2 shallots, chopped
2 × 15ml spoons/2 tablespoons each chopped
  parsley and onion
1 clove garlic, peeled and chopped
1 × 15ml spoon/1 tablespoon chopped chives
5 anchovy fillets, drained, dried and finely
  chopped
25g/1 oz butter
300ml/½ pint red wine

Nick the skin of the meat to prevent curling and sprinkle with peppercorns
and dried thyme. Rub these and the cut halves of garlic well into the meat on
both sides. Roughly chop the garlic, mix with the parsley, and press
into the meat.
Spread half the vegetables in a small earthenware dish, put the meat on top
and cover with the remainder.
Beat the vinegar and oil together until cloudy, beat in the wine and pour
down the sides of the dish. Cover and leave overnight in a cool place. Do not
chill. Turn once during this time.
Transfer the meat to a *cocotte* and strain the marinade over it, discarding the
vegetables. Cover and bring to boiling over low heat. Simmer for 1½ hours
on top of the cooker or cook at 170°C/325°F/Gas 3 in the oven for slightly
longer. Turn the meat over once.
For the sauce, chop the shallots, parsley, onion, garlic and chives to a fine
paste. Pound the anchovies with the butter until creamy, form into a
roll and chill.
Remove the meat and wipe out the pan. Pour in the wine, add the shallot
mixture, stir well and replace the meat. Cover and simmer over low heat for
15 minutes.
Transfer the meat to a serving dish, cover closely with foil and keep hot.
Remove the pan from the heat and with a hand whisk beat in the anchovy
butter in small pieces. When thickened pour the sauce over the meat cut into
4 pieces, and serve with boiled potatoes.

Estouffade de Boeuf à la Niçoise
Beef in White Wine, Tomato and Herb Sauce

Serves 6

In Provence, where the quality of the olives, their oil and the huge locally grown tomatoes is far superior to that of the local red wine, beef is cooked with herbs and these vegetables in a light white wine to produce a fine aromatic dish.

225g/8oz pickled belly pork (see page 37), cut into lardons
3 × 15ml spoons/3 tablespoons olive oil
1kg/2 lb chuck steak, cut very thick and cubed
2 large onions, quartered
2 × 15ml spoons/2 tablespoons flour
2 × 5 ml spoons/2 tablespoons coarse sea salt
black pepper

750ml/1¼ pints dry white wine
300ml/½ pint water
1 clove garlic, halved
1 bouquet garni (see page 14)
2 cloves
6 Mediterranean tomatoes or 12 large domestic ones, de-seeded and halved
24 small black olives, stoned
1 × 15ml spoon/1 tablespoon chopped parsley

Blanch the lardons for 5 minutes and drain on absorbent paper. Heat the oil in a frying pan and over medium heat brown first the lardons, then the meat on all sides, then each onion separately. Drain.

Stir the flour into the fats, season and mix well. Add the wine, water, garlic, herbs and cloves. Return browned ingredients to the pan and bring slowly to boiling. Cover, reduce heat to very low and simmer for 1½ hours.

Remove the meat, onions and lardons from the pan and place in a clean *cocotte* or braising pan, cover with the tomatoes placed cut side down and arrange the olives on top.

Strain the cooking liquid into a wide-topped bowl and skim off excess fat. Pour the liquids over the meat, cover and simmer for a further 40 minutes after boiling point is reached. Remove the lid for the last 10 minutes to reduce the sauce.

Pour the *estouffade* into a deep, heated serving dish, sprinkle with chopped parsley and serve with boiled potatoes.

Note This dish is excellent reheated and is also good for freezing.

Côtes de Veau Normande
Veal Chops with Apples, Cream and Calvados

Serves 6

The lush pastures of Normandy produce fine cattle, thick cream, apples and calvados. When they are combined to celebrate a special occasion they produce a memorable dish.

150g/5 oz butter
6 thick veal chops with bone, about 225g/8 oz
* each*
salt, black pepper, sugar
300ml/½ pint double cream

6 × 15ml spoons/6 tablespoons calvados
* (apple brandy)*
1kg/2 lb dessert apples, peeled, cored and cut
* into 8*

Heat half the butter in a *sauteuse* or large frying pan over medium low heat and colour the chops golden brown on both sides. Place them in a shallow ovenproof dish just large enough to hold them, season well, cover closely with foil and place in the oven at 180°C/350°F/Gas 4 on the middle shelf. Deglaze the pan with cream, scraping the base to release the meat juices, heat until simmering and reduce by a third. Add the calvados, mix well, pour over the meat, cover again and cook for 30 minutes or until tender.

Wipe out the pan. Heat the remaining butter over medium heat, and when foaming cook the apple slices golden on both sides. Sprinkle lightly with sugar and glaze on both sides, shaking the pan frequently to prevent sticking. Remove from the heat and cover.

Arrange the chops on a heated serving dish, check seasoning of the sauce and pour it over the chops. Place the apple slices around the dish and serve with buttered noodles or Riz au Blanc (page 40).

Côtes de Veau Normande with Riz au Blanc
(page 40)

Tendron de Veau à la Provençale
Breast of Veal with Tomatoes

Serves 6

---

3 × 15ml spoons/3 tablespoons olive oil
1.5 kg/3 lb breast of veal, cut into 2.5cm/
  1 inch thick slices
2 medium sized onions, finely chopped
1 large shallot, finely chopped
1 piece dried orange peel
5 Mediterranean tomatoes or 10 large
  domestic tomatoes, skinned, de-seeded and
  chopped

1 bouquet garni (see page 14)
2 cloves garlic, crushed
1 × 15ml spoon/1 tablespoon concentrated
  tomato purée
150ml/¼ pint dry white wine
salt, black pepper, cayenne

Heat the oil in a *sauteuse* over moderate heat and colour the meat. Remove from the pan and keep warm between two plates. Cook the onions, shallot and orange peel in the same oil, until the onions are tender, without colouring.

Add tomato flesh, herbs, garlic and tomato purée. Pour in the wine and mix until smooth. Add the meat, seasoning and a big pinch of cayenne. Cover and leave to simmer over low heat for approximately 1½ hours.

The sauce should be thick when cooked, but if it becomes too thick before the meat is tender, add boiling water, a tablespoonful at a time.

Serve with buttered noodles (see page 42).

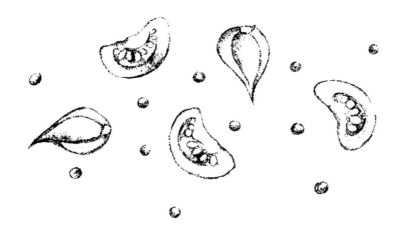

Ragoût D'Agneau
Ragoût of Lamb with Potatoes and Herbs

Serves 4-6

700g/1½ lb lean shoulder of lamb, cut into serving pieces
700g/1½ lb neck of lamb, chopped into joint pieces
1 × 5ml spoon/1 teaspoon salt
2.5ml/½ teaspoon black pepper
7.5ml/1½ teaspoons sugar
1 × 15ml spoon/1 tablespoon pure lard
2 × 15ml spoons/2 tablespoons flour

4 × 15ml spoons/4 tablespoons concentrated tomato purée
1 litre/1¾ pints water
1 bouquet garni (see page 14)
15g/½ oz butter
20 small onions (pickling size)
20 small new potatoes, scraped
1 × 15ml spoon/1 tablespoon chopped parsley

Sprinkle the meat with salt, pepper and 2.5ml/½ teaspoon sugar. Leave to impregnate for 10 minutes.

Heat the lard in a *cocotte* or frying pan and colour the meat golden brown over moderately low heat.

Pour off excess fat, sprinkle meat with flour, stir it around the pan to coat and allow to colour slightly. Dissolve the tomato purée in the water and pour over the meat. Scrape up the meat juices on the base of the pan and stir them into the sauce. Add bouquet garni and seasoning. Cover and leave to simmer over low heat for 1½ hours.

Heat the butter in a frying pan and sauté the onions, shaking the pan to coat on all sides. Sprinkle with the remaining sugar and allow to glaze until golden. Remove the bouquet garni from the pan, add the onions and potatoes, cover and cook gently for a further 30 minutes.

To serve, skim off excess fat from the surface of the liquid, return the liquid to the pan and reheat. Sprinkle with parsley and serve immediately.

Note If the lard darkens during the sauté process empty the pan, wipe it out and start again.

If prepared in a frying pan cooking can be completed in the oven. Transfer to a casserole and cook at 170°C/325°F/Gas 3 for 1½ hours.

This dish reheats well. Reheat in the oven at 180°C/350°F/Gas 4 for 35–40 minutes with fresh potatoes, previously par-boiled for 5 minutes.

Gigot d'Auvergne en Cocotte
Braised Leg of Lamb with Onions

Serves 8

The frugality of the Auvergnian peasant is legendary. They find it no hardship to eat their native chestnuts as a main course instead of meat. But when on special occasions they cook a leg of lamb it is memorable.

2 cloves
8 large flat onions
25g/1 oz butter
12 shallots
4 white peppercorns, crushed
6 black peppercorns

salt, grated nutmeg, powered ginger and
  allspice
1 sprig thyme
1 bay leaf
2kg/4 lb leg of spring lamb, or shoulder
8 medium sized potatoes
150ml/¼ pint dry white wine

Stick the cloves into two of the onions.

Thickly butter a large iron *cocotte*, a *Doufeu* or braising pan with half the butter, spread the onions in one layer and add the shallots, peppercorns, salt, two generous pinches each nutmeg, ginger and allspice. Add the herbs.

Make 3 deep cuts in the thickest part of the meat and rub a nut of the remaining butter and a big pinch of spices into each one. Place the meat on top of the vegetables. Cover, and if a *Doufeu* is used, fill the sunken lid with cold water. Place over medium heat and when the contents of the pan sing, lower heat immediately and cook for 1 hour, turning the meat over once. If the onions stick add more butter.

Season the potatoes lightly and put in with the meat. Add the wine, cover and cook for a further 30–40 minutes, then transfer meat and vegetables to a shallow ovenproof dish and place under a low grill about 15cm/6 inches below the element. Leave for 15 minutes to brown.

To serve, carve the meat across the bone into thick slices. Arrange these on a heated serving dish surrounded by the vegetables.

Strain the liquids into a sauce boat and hand separately.

Gigot d'Auvergne en Cocotte

POULTRY & GAME

The meadows of the Bresse region are thickly speckled with fat white hens and capons, each one a peer of its realm. These birds are hand-raised and famous throughout France for the delicacy of their flesh. Guinea fowl too are fed with special care to produce tender juicy meat whose flavour, slightly reminiscent of pheasant, is much appreciated by amateurs of game.

Another favourite is domestic rabbit. As cooked in the French kitchen, it is a great delicacy. In the Midi, rabbits are fed on sprigs of savory or rosemary to aromatize the flesh.

Petits Poussins au Citron
Spring Chickens with Lemon

Serves 4

2 poussins, 450g/1 lb each, skinned and quartered, livers reserved
salt, black pepper
2 large lemons, zest finely chopped, juice squeezed

2 × 15ml spoons/2 tablespoons olive oil
2 × 15ml spoons/2 tablespoons soy sauce
1 clove garlic, crushed

Poach the chicken livers in salted water for 1 minute, drain.
Place chicken pieces in a shallow dish, flesh side down. Beat half the lemon juice into the olive oil, add soy sauce, peel and garlic. Season, beat well with a hand whisk and pour over the chicken, pressing the peel into the meat on both sides. Leave for 2 hours to marinate. Baste occasionally.
Heat the grill to maximum. Place the chicken underneath in its marinade, about 13cm/5 inches below the element. Cook for 10 minutes. Turn the pieces over, sprinkle with the remaining lemon juice, baste and press the peel into the surface. Reduce the heat and grill for 10 minutes until the meat is tender, crisp and brown. Remove to a heated serving dish and keep hot.
Crush the livers into the pan juices, beat well, pour over the chicken and serve immediately.

Poulet Bertrand
Chicken in Cream and Brandy

Serves 6

This chicken dish, very popular in Anjou, is cooked with the best of white wine and brandy to produce a particularly delicious sauce.

*1 roasting chicken, 2 kg/4 lb, cut into serving
  pieces
40g/1½ oz salted butter
40g/1½ oz unsalted butter
salt, black pepper*

*150ml/¼ pint dry white wine
3 × 15ml spoons/3 tablespoons brandy
2 large egg yolks, beaten
300ml/½ pint double cream*

Pull off any fat inside the chicken and render it down over gentle heat in a *sauteuse* or large frying pan. Add the salted butter and when hot brown the chicken pieces on both sides. Drain on absorbent paper.

Pour away the fats, wipe out the pan and heat the unsalted butter. Replace the chicken, season well and sauté over increased heat for 2–3 minutes.

Pour in the wine and brandy, stir, and draw the pan from the heat. Ignite immediately and baste the meat until the flames die out. Cover closely, reduce heat to low and simmer for 1 hour.

To serve, arrange the chicken on a heated dish, cover and keep hot. Scrape the base of the pan to release meat juices, bring to boiling point and remove from heat. Beat the egg yolks and cream together and blend into the sauce. The pan can be replaced over heat during this process but *do not let the sauce boil*.

Pour it over the chicken and serve with buttered noodles.

Poulet au Riz à la Ménagère
Chicken with Rice

Serves 8

The countrywoman's simple method of cooking the Sunday chicken in a big pot with rice, plenty of vegetables and herbs is the recipe that was perfected by Escoffier, although I doubt whether his humble followers are aware of the fact.

salt, black pepper
1 roasting chicken, 2 kg/4 lb
200ml/⅓ pint cold water
1.5 litres/2½ pints hot water
15g/½ oz coarse sea salt
4 small onions
2 cloves

1 heart of celery
225g/8 oz small carrots, scraped and thinly sliced
1 bouquet garni (see page 14)
100g/4 oz rice, washed and drained
50g/2 oz butter, cut into small pieces

Season the bird inside, place in a large soup pan and pour in the cold water. Cover and place over medium heat. Leave for 10 minutes until the water has evaporated completely.
Add the hot water and sea salt and bring slowly to boiling point. Skim off the froth as it rises.
When boiling steadily, add the onions (2 stuck with cloves), vegetables, herbs and some pepper. Reduce the heat, cover and simmer for 1 hour 10 minutes. Scatter the rice around the chicken, increase the heat slightly and when boiling again, cover and cook for 15 minutes more, or until the rice is tender. Remove the chicken carefully from the pan and place in a deep serving dish. Cover and keep hot. Remove the bouquet garni and cloves from the pan. Stir in the butter gently, piece by piece, then pour the vegetables, rice and liquid around the chicken.
Serve at once with a bottle of chilled Vouvray.

Pintades à l'Ancienne
Old-fashioned Casserole of Guinea-hen

Serves 6

225g/8 oz lean streaky bacon in one piece, rind removed, meat cut into lardons
2 medium sized carrots, peeled and diced
1 small young turnip, peeled and diced
12 small onions
2 guinea hens, 1kg/2 lb each, quartered
1 × 15ml spoon/1 tablespoon flour
4 × 15ml spoons/4 tablespoons water
150ml/¼ pint dry white wine
225g/8 oz button mushrooms, wiped, trimmed and dried
salt, black pepper
2 × 15ml spoons/2 tablespoons double cream
juice of ½ lemon

Put the lardons into a *cocotte* over medium heat and leave to render the fat, stirring occasionally. When coloured, add carrots, turnips and onions and colour lightly. Remove and drain on absorbent paper.

Turn the pieces of guinea-hen over in the fat, and when coloured, sprinkle with flour. Cook and stir for a few minutes. Pour the water and wine mixed into the *cocotte* and add the browned vegetables and the mushrooms. Season well, cover and simmer over low heat for about 1½ hours, until tender.

To serve, pile the meat in the centre of a deep serving dish, arrange the vegetables around it, cover and keep hot.

Bind the juices with the cream, add a few drops of lemon juice to sharpen the flavour, check seasoning and pour over the birds.

Serve with floury boiled potatoes.

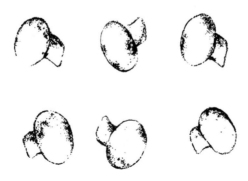

Lapin au Chou
Rabbit with Cabbage

Serves 4–5

---

*225g/8 oz pickled belly of pork (see page 57),
rind removed, meat cut into lardons
25g/1 oz pork dripping
1 young rabbit, 1.5kg/3 lb, cut into serving
pieces
4 medium sized onions, sliced*

*2 carrots, peeled and sliced
1.2kg/2½ lb firm-hearted green cabbage,
trimmed and quartered, core removed
salt, black pepper
150ml/¼ pint warm water*

Blanch the lardons for 3 minutes, drain and dry.
Melt the dripping in a large frying pan and colour the rabbit on both sides to golden brown. As the pieces colour, remove from the pan and drain. Add the lardons, lower the heat and colour them lightly.
Add the onions and carrots and colour until golden brown, stirring frequently. Blanch the cabbage for 3 minutes only, drain and squeeze dry.
In a *cocotte* or casserole, place a layer of cabbage, season lightly, cover with rabbit, a layer of pork and vegetables and so on until the *cocotte* is full, ending with a layer of cabbage and a sprinkling of pork and vegetables. Add the warm water, cover closely and place over very low heat. When boiling, simmer for about 1 hour 15 minutes without lifting the lid.
Should a great deal of liquid remain when the meat is tender, reduce, uncovered, for about 5–6 minutes.
Serve with potatoes boiled in their skins.

Note If this dish is cooked in the oven, allow 1¾–2 hours at 170°C/325°F/ Gas 3 and place the dish in the lower half.

VEGETABLES

French country people grow few flowers. 'You can't eat them,' as one farmer succinctly explained. But his wife will spare a little time to cultivate a few geraniums, marguerites and begonias around her kitchen door. Her main occupation apart from the chickens and rabbits is helping in the market garden.

Vegetables and salads are an important and delicious part of the French diet. That is why they are served as a separate course.

Oignons a l'Orientale
Spiced Onions

Serve as a first course

Sundays on a French farm mean an especially good lunch. No work in the afternoon gives plenty of time to enjoy a first course, as well as a sweet dish, both of them treats not indulged in at weekday meals. Vegetable first courses are very popular.

1kg/2 lb small silver-skinned onions or pickling onions
salt, black pepper, saffron
approx. 300ml/½ pint dry white wine
approx. 4 × 15ml spoons/4 tablespoons olive oil

3 large Mediterranean tomatoes or 6 large domestic tomatoes, skinned, de-seeded and chopped
1 clove garlic, chopped
6 coriander seeds, crushed

Arrange the onions in one layer in a wide-based pan or a *sauteuse* and sprinkle with salt. Beat the wine and oil together until cloudy and pour over the onions to barely cover. Add more if necessary. Spread the tomatoes over the onions. Season, add garlic, coriander, and two generous pinches of saffron. The latter flavour should predominate.

Cover, place over low heat and, when boiling, reduce to minimum and cook until the onions are tender.

Leave until cold, pour into a large screw-topped jar and store chilled.

To serve, drain the number required, about 5–6 per person, and serve with sliced and buttered rye bread.

Aubergines aux Trois Fromages
Aubergines with Three Cheeses

Serves 4 as a main course

The market gardeners of Provence, whose most important crops are aubergines, tomatoes and courgettes, have innumerable ways of cooking their produce. This recipe holds all the savours of the Midi.

1kg/2 lb aubergines, thinly peeled and sliced 5mm/¼ inch thick
salt, black pepper
4–5 × 15ml spoons/4–5 tablespoons olive oil

175g/6 oz curd cheese
100g/4 oz Gruyère cheese, grated
75g/3 oz Parmesan cheese, grated
150g/5 oz can tomato purée

Sprinkle the aubergines liberally with salt on both sides and place between two large plates with a weight on top. After 1 hour drain, wash and dry them. Heat half the oil in a frying pan over medium heat and brown half the aubergines. Remove from the pan and drain on absorbent paper. Heat remaining oil and brown and drain the rest.

Place a layer of aubergines in a gratin dish, season with pepper only and dot with pieces of curd cheese. Sprinkle with some of both the other cheeses and continue in this order until the dish is full, ending with the two grated cheeses.

Mix the tomato purée with 3 cansful of hot water, mix and pour down the sides of the dish.

Bake for 45 minutes at 180°C/350°F/Gas 4. Increase the heat to 200°C/400°F/Gas 6 and cook until crusted and brown.

Serve immediately.

Note Buy Gruyère and Parmesan cheese in whole pieces: they have much more flavour when grated as required. Buy the curd cheese loose from the delicatessen – the commercial variety in cartons is not suitable for this recipe.

Bouillabaisse Borgne
Vegetable Bouillabaisse

Serves 4 as a main course

Some of the old French country dishes have very strange names, like this one known as One-eyed Bouillabaisse. The distinction of being one-eyed comes from the poached egg served on top.

12 walnut halves
4 × 15ml spoons/4 tablespoons olive oil
2 large leeks, cut into short lengths, green included
2 medium-large onions, quartered
1 clove garlic
peel of ½ small orange
4 large Mediterranean tomatoes or 8 large domestic tomatoes, skinned and cut into 8 pieces
1 bouquet garni (see page 14)

salt, black pepper, saffron
1 litre/1¾ pints hot water
450g/1 lb waxy red-skinned potatoes, thickly sliced
1 × 15ml spoon/1 tablespoon vinegar
600ml/1 pint water
4 large eggs
4 thin slices stale rye bread
1 × 15ml spoon/1 tablespoon parsley, chopped

Crush the walnuts into the oil in a mortar or with a wooden spoon. Stir together in a large pan over medium heat, and when hot add leeks, onions and garlic and cook until well coloured. Add orange peel, tomatoes, herbs, seasoning and a generous pinch of saffron. Pour on the hot water, stir well over low heat and bring to boiling, but do not cover.

Add potato slices (halved if very large) and cook until tender.

Boil the vinegar and water in a frying pan and poach the eggs.

To serve, remove bouquet garni and orange peel from the pan and put a slice of bread in each of 4 deep, heated soup plates. Ladle the bouillabaisse over them and place a poached egg on top.

Sprinkle with parsley and serve immediately.

Champignons à l'Aïl
Mushrooms with Garlic and Sausagemeat

Serves 4 as a supper dish

When very large field mushrooms can be found they make a remarkably good dish if cooked with a few good pork sausages or home-made sausagemeat.

4–5 large cloves garlic, chopped
1kg/2 lb open field mushrooms, peeled, stalks removed and trimmed
4 country pork sausages or approx 225g/8 oz home-made sausagemeat
3 × 15ml spoons/3 tablespoons chopped parsley

salt, black pepper
2 × 15ml spoons/2 tablespoons olive oil
50g/2 oz butter
3 thick slices bread, crusts removed, cut into 2.5cm/1 inch wide strips

Chop the garlic and mushrooms stalks finely together. If using sausages, remove the skins. Add the sausagemeat to the garlic mixture. Mix in parsley and seasoning.

Heat the oil in a wide, shallow *cocotte* and place in it a layer of mushrooms, season lightly and cover with a layer of garlic mixture. Continue layering, seasoning each layer of mushrooms lightly, cover with a sheet of buttered greaseproof paper over the rim, sprinkle with drops of cold water and force the lid over it. Cook over minimum heat for 1–1½ hours, lifting the lid at 30 minute intervals.

Add 15–30ml/1–2 tablespoons water if the juices have been absorbed.

Bring butter to foaming over medium heat in a frying pan and fry the bread golden brown. Drain on absorbent paper and keep hot.

To serve, stand the croûtons round the inside of the *cocotte* and serve immediately.

Chou Rouge Limousin
Red Cabbage with Chestnuts and Red Wine

Serves 8–10

In the farms of the Limousin area this dish of red cabbage is made in large quantities because it is almost better reheated than when cooked the first time. On special occasions it is served with roast pork, or for family meals with grilled sausages.

100g/4 oz pickled pork (see page 57), cut into lardons
1 large onion, chopped
1.5kg/3 lb red cabbage, trimmed, quartered and shredded
2 × 15ml spoons/2 tablespoons wine vinegar

200ml/⅓ pint red wine
2.5ml/½ teaspoon each salt, ground cloves and grated nutmeg
1kg/2 lb chestnuts, skinned and peeled if fresh, drained if canned (use the unsweetened variety)

Blanch the lardons for 5 minutes. drain and dry.
Heat a large *cocotte* over low heat for a few moments and sauté the lardons until they render their fat and are coloured on all sides.
Add the onion, mix into the fat and brown lightly. Add the cabbage and mix well. Cover and cook over low heat for 10 minutes. Add the lardons, vinegar, wine, salt, cloves and a pinch of grated nutmeg. Mix again, cover and cook over minimum heat for 2 hours, stirring occasionally.
Peel the chestnuts and add to the cabbage after cooking for 2 hours. Stir them in, check seasoning, cover and cook very slowly for 1 hour more.

Note This dish can be cooked in a casserole in the oven at 170°C/325°F/Gas 3 after all the ingredients except the cabbage have been prepared in a large frying pan.
To reheat, cover closely with foil. Place in a bain-marie in the oven at 190°C/375°F/Gas 5 for approx 30 minutes.
To skin chestnuts, slit on rounded side, place in baking tin in 1cm/½ inch water and put in a hot oven for 10 minutes. If skins do not peel easily, cover with a damp cloth for 5 minutes, then peel.

Courgettes Provençale
Courgettes with Tomatoes, Cheese and Garlic

Serves 4

Provençal people serve the following dish of courgettes accompanied by plain boiled rice as a main course in place of meat.

2 cloves garlic, crushed
2 × 15ml spoons/2 tablespoons olive oil
750g/1½ lb courgettes, unpeeled and thickly sliced slant-wise
1 large onion, chopped
4 Mediterranean tomatoes or 8 large domestic tomatoes, skinned, de-seeded and chopped
2.5ml/½ teaspoon dried thyme

salt, black pepper
2 × 15ml spoons/2 tablespoons chopped parsley
100g/4 oz Gruyère cheese, grated
4 × 15ml spoons/4 tablespoons dry white wine
chapelure (see page 13)

Put the garlic and oil into a large frying pan and cook over gentle heat. Put in one layer of courgettes and cook long enough to soften slightly. Remove and keep warm. Half-cook the rest in the same way. In the same oil cook the onion, and when transparent add tomato flesh and thyme, mix well and cook for about 30 minutes until reduced to a thick consistency. Season and stir in the chopped parsley.

Butter a shallow ovenproof dish and cover with half the courgettes. Season and cover with half the cheese and half the tomato mixture, cover with the rest of the ingredients in the same order. Pour the wine down the sides of the dish, sprinkle thickly with *chapelure* and bake for 30–40 minutes at 200°C/400°F/Gas 6 until bubbling and brown on top.

Serve immediately with Riz au Blanc (see page 40).

Fèves à la Crème
Broad Beans with Cream and Herbs

Serves 4

All vegetables in France are picked very small, when tender and their flavour is at its best. Young broad beans, cooked with herbs and cream, are especially good served with a thick slice of cold boiled ham.

1kg/2 lb young broad beans, shelled
40g/1½ oz butter
salt, black pepper

2 × 15ml spoons/2 tablespoons chopped
chervil, tarragon, savory or chives
4 × 15ml spoons/4 tablespoons double cream

Cook the beans in just enough boiling salted water to cover. When tender, drain, and put the dry pan back over medium heat. Melt the butter, add the beans, season well, and sauté them for a few minutes. Shake pan so that the contents do not colour. Add the herbs, sauté again to mix well and stir in the cream carefully.
Check the seasoning and when hot, pour into a heated serving dish and serve immediately.

Gratin de Poireaux
Leeks with Gruyère Cheese and Bacon

Serves 4

750g/1½ lb small leeks, cleaned, green part
retained, cut into 5cm/2 inch lengths
15g/½ oz butter
salt, black pepper

175g/6 oz Gruyère cheese, grated
175g/6 oz lean bacon rashers, chopped and
rind removed
250ml/8 fl oz chicken bouillon (see page 18)

Blanch the leeks for approx. 5 minutes until not quite cooked. Drain well and squeeze out excess moisture.
Coat a gratin or other ovenproof dish with butter, arrange a layer of leeks in the base, season, sprinkle with cheese and scraps of bacon and cover with another layer of leeks. Fill the dish in this way and sprinkle the remaining cheese over the surface.
Pour the bouillon down the sides of the dish and bake at 180°C/350°F/Gas 4 for about 35 minutes, until the leeks are tender and the cheese browned on top. Serve immediately.

Pommes de Terre au Lard
Potato Casserole with Bacon

Serves 4

15g/½ oz butter
225g/8 oz lean streaky bacon in one piece, cut
    into lardons
1 medium onion, coarsely chopped
1 clove garlic, chopped
450g/1 lb large tomatoes, preferably
    Mediterranean variety, skinned and
    chopped

1 bouquet garni (see page 14)
1kg/2 lb potatoes, thickly sliced
300ml/½ pint bouillon (see page 18)
salt and pepper
2 × 5ml spoons/2 teaspoons flour (optional)
1 × 15ml spoon/1 tablespoon water (optional)

Heat the butter in a heavy pan over low heat, add the lardons and sauté until they start to colour. Add the onion and garlic and cook until golden brown. Add the tomatoes and cook together for 5 minutes, stirring constantly. Add the herbs, potatoes and bouillon and season well. Increase the heat to medium and cook until the potatoes are tender.
Check seasoning. Remove the bouquet garni before serving. Serve very hot with plenty of crisp French bread.

Le Petatou
Soufflé Potatoes with Curd Cheese

Serves 4

450g/1 lb floury potatoes, quartered if large
salt, black pepper
2 large eggs, separated

50g/2 oz butter
2–3 × 15ml spoons/2–3 tablespoons milk
100g/4 oz curd cheese

Boil the potatoes in salted water until tender.
Add a pinch of salt to the egg whites and beat until stiff. Chill.
Heat the oven to 200°C/400°F/Gas 6.
Drain the potatoes, put them into a heated bowl, season highly, add the butter cut into small pieces and mix thoroughly. Mash down and beat with a hand whisk or blend. Mix just enough milk with the cheese to form a thick cream and beat into the potatoes. Beat in the egg yolks. Beat the whites again until very stiff and *fold* into the potato mixture. Do not beat or stir.
Pour into a buttered ovenproof dish and bake until well risen and golden brown on top, about 20–25 minutes. Serve without delay.

SWEET DISHES & SPECIAL FRUIT TARTS

In the French repertory, sweet dishes are more than just sweet. They all have an additional, subtle flavour, and even the simple homely ones serve to emphasize the fact that Sunday is a day of leisure on the farm. This subtlety may be imparted by rum, brandy, liqueur or vanilla. The tart for special occasions (*la tarte de cérémonie*) is made at home by country people. They prefer their own family recipes for these events to the excellent classic fruit tarts made by the *patissier*.

Flan aux Raisins
Grape Flan

Serves 6

225g/8 oz frozen puff pastry, thawed for 1 hour at room temperature
450g/1 lb large green grapes, washed, picked over and drained
225g/8 oz large black grapes, washed, picked over and drained
2 medium sized eggs, beaten

100g/4 oz caster sugar
3 × 15ml spoons/3 tablespoons ground almonds
100ml/4 fl oz double cream
(a 25cm/10 inch flan tin with loose base, buttered and floured)

Heat the oven to 230°C/450°F/Gas 8 with a baking sheet on middle shelf. Roll out pastry thinly and line tin. Chill until required. Dry grapes on absorbent paper and arrange them closely over pastry. Beat eggs and sugar together until thick, beat in the ground almonds and finally the cream.
Spread evenly over grapes and bake for 20 minutes. Reduce heat to 200°C/400°F/Gas 6 and bake for another 20 minutes.
If the surface browns too quickly, balance a sheet of foil on top. Cool for 5 minutes on a wire tray. Serve warm.

Flan Aux Raisins

Cerises à l'Eau-de-Vie
Morello Cherries in Liqueur

Many Frenchmen (all self-appointed wine experts), never eat sweet dishes on the pretext that sugar affects the delicacy of their palate, but they never refuse Cerises à l'Eau-de-Vie served with black coffee as an alternative.

About 1kg/2 lb ripe morello or sour cherries, washed and dried

350g/12 oz caster sugar
1 litre/1¾ pints alcohol, 65·5°

Discard any cherries that are bruised and cut down the stalk to 1cm/½ inch. Pierce each one with a darning needle in two places and put into a large wide-topped glass jar, layering the fruit and sugar until they are used up.
Fill up with alcohol, cork tightly, seal with wax and leave on a sunny window sill for at least 2 months, turning and shaking the jar carefully from time to time.
Serve in small glasses, 3 or 4 cherries for each person, just covered with liqueur.

Note The *eau-de-vie* or *alcool à fruits* sold by every village grocer in France is unobtainable elsewhere, but vodka is a perfect substitute.

Fraises à la Crème
Strawberries, Liqueur and Cream

Serves 4–5

450g/1 lb strawberries, washed, dried and hulled, halved if large
4 × 15ml spoons/4 tablespoons caster sugar

4 × 15ml spoons/4 tablespoons curaçao or cherry brandy
300ml/½ pint double cream
2 dry macaroons

Place the fruit in a wide serving bowl and sprinkle with half the sugar. Cover and leave in a cool place (do not chill), for 1 hour. Add the liqueur, cover and leave for 2 hours.
When ready to serve, if the cream is liquid whisk it until thick with the remaining sugar and mix with fruit. Use two forks to avoid crushing it.
Serve lightly chilled with the macaroons crumbled on the surface.

Charlotte aux Pommes
Apple Charlotte with White Wine

Serves 4–6

---

*1kg/2 lb dessert apples, peeled, cored and
  sliced
juice of 1 lemon
60g/2½ oz unsalted butter
150ml/¼ pint white wine, sweet or dry*

*2 × 15ml spoons/2 tablespoons sugar
1 vanilla pod
1 stale white loaf, 450g/1 lb, sliced 3 mm/¼
  inch thick
(a 1 litre/2 pint charlotte mould)*

Drop the apple slices into a bowl of cold water with lemon juice added to
prevent discoloration.

Heat 50g/2 oz butter in a *sauteuse* or large frying pan over low heat, add the
wine, sugar and vanilla pod and bring very slowly to boiling point. Dry the
apples and cook slowly in the wine until tender. Remove, drain and reserve
the juices.

Wash and dry the vanilla pod for future use.

Coat the mould thickly with the remaining butter, line the base with paper
and cover with a circle of bread. Line *closely* with bread cut into long fingers
4 cm/1½ inches wide, dipped on one side only in the pan juices. Do not trim
excess. Fill with apple, cover with circle of dipped bread and fold upstanding
ends over it. Press down firmly and bake in the centre of the oven at 200°C/
400°F/Gas 6 for 1 hour, or until sides show golden brown when pressed
inwards with a knife. Cook for another 15–20 minutes if not.

To unmould, loosen completely with a knife, place a heated plate on top,
invert and set down with a sharp tap. Serve with thick cream.

Mousse Glacée au Rhum
Iced Rum Mousse

Serves 6–8

---

4 large eggs, separated
150g/6 oz caster sugar

4 × 15ml spoons/4 tablespoons dark rum
300ml/½ pint double cream, beaten thick

Beat the egg yolks, sugar and rum with a hand whisk and pour into a double boiler. Cook, stirring constantly over low heat, until the mixture drops from the spoon in a thick ribbon. Pour into a mixing bowl, and stir until cold. Beat the egg whites to a stiff peak. *Beat* the cream into the egg mixture and *fold* in the whites a third at a time. Freeze for 8 hours.
To serve, scoop into chilled glasses and serve with boudoir biscuits.

Gâteau au Fromage Blanc
Hot Cheesecake

Serves 6

---

3 large eggs, separated, yolks beaten
salt
350g/12 oz curd cheese
5 × 15ml spoons/5 tablespoons caster sugar
grated rind of 1 lemon
4 × 15ml spoons/4 tablespoons flour

grated rind of 1 orange
2 × 15ml spoons/2 tablespoons finely chopped
candied orange and lemon peel
(a cake tin, 15cm/6 inches diameter × 5cm/2
inches deep, buttered and floured)

Preheat the oven to 190°C/375°F/Gas 5.
Put the yolks and a pinch of salt into one bowl and 2 whites into another. Mix the cheese into the egg yolks and beat with a hand whisk or blend until smooth. Stir in the sugar until dissolved, then gradually add lemon rind and sifted flour. Beat or blend until smooth. Stir in orange rind and candied peels.
Beat the whites to a stiff peak and *fold* them in, a third at a time.
Pour this mixture into the cake tin, bake for 30 minutes, then increase the heat to 200°C/400°F/Gas 6 and cook for another 1 hour or until the centre is set and a skewer plunged into it comes out clean. Remove from the oven and leave for 5 minutes before unmoulding as advised on page 89.
Sprinkle with caster sugar and serve warm with thick cream.

Mousse Glacé au Rhum

Poires Grillées au Miel
Pears Grilled with Honey

Serves 4

Country fruit dishes are usually very simple, quite enough for ending a large Sunday lunch – more as a full stop than an entire sentence.

4 large ripe William pears, washed, dried and halved
juice of 1 lemon, strained
25g/1 oz unsalted butter, melted

approx. 1 × 15ml spoon/1 tablespoon honey
approx. 1 × 15ml spoon/1 tablespoon sugar
100ml/4 fl oz double cream, whipped and chilled

Hollow out the core of the pears with a teaspoon, making a cavity. Pour 5ml/1 teaspoon lemon juice into the hollow and brush the cut surface with it. Arrange the pears head to tail and cut side down in a flameproof dish, pour the rest of the lemon juice into the dish and set aside until 20 minutes before serving.
Heat the grill to maximum.
Brush the pears with butter and place them under the grill, about 10cm/4 inches from the element. Grill for 7–8 minutes. Turn them over, brush with butter again, and fill the hollows with honey. Trail a thread of it over the surface, sprinkle thickly with sugar and replace under the grill for 8–10 minutes, until brown.
Allow to cool a little. Place a spoonful of cream on each pear and serve warm with the juices from the dish poured over the cream.

Tarte Frangipane aux Cerises
Almond and Cherry Tart

Serves 6

In this tart, the sharp flavour of morello cherries contrast deliciously with the sweet almond filling.

pâte sucrée for 6–8 (see page 33)
(a 25cm/10 inch flan tin with a loose base)
FILLING
125g/4½ oz unsalted butter, creamed
125g/4½ oz sugar
125g/4½ oz ground almonds
1 × 5ml spoon/1 teaspoon flour
2 large eggs
2 × 15ml spoons/2 tablespoons rum

450g/1 lb morello cherries (fresh or canned),
* stoned*
GLAZE
175g/6 oz icing sugar
1 × 15ml spoon/1 tablespoon rum
2 × 15ml spoons/2 tablespoons water
redcurrant jelly

Butter the flan tin. Roll out the pastry to 5mm/¼ inch thick. Line the tin, and if the pastry breaks, press together with the fingertips. Trim the edges, prick the base with a fork and chill for 30 minutes.

Heat the oven to 200°C/400°F/Gas 6, with a baking sheet on the middle shelf. Drop the butter into a warmed bowl, add the sugar, ground almonds and flour, and beat with a hand whisk to a smooth cream.

Add the eggs one at a time, beat in thoroughly, then stir in the rum. Arrange the cherries in the bottom of the pastry case and pour the cream evenly over them.

Bake for about 30 minutes, or until coloured pale golden. Cover lightly with foil and continue baking. Count 1 hour 10 minutes baking time in all. Remove from the oven and place on a wire tray.

Dissolve the icing sugar, rum and water in a small pan over low heat, beating constantly with a hand whisk. Melt some redcurrant jelly to a spreading consistency. Brush the surface of the tart with jelly, pour the glaze over it and smooth evenly with a metal spatula.

Serve either warm or cold.

Note If morellos are unobtainable, red dessert cherries can be used, but they should not be too sweet.

Meals & Menu Planning

The French farmworker eats a hearty mid-day meal.

From 12 noon to 1.30 he enjoys a rest, a robust main course of meat and fresh vegetables, a few glasses of his local wine, a green salad, with cheese and fruit to end this well-balanced meal. The tempting first course of pâté or spiced vegetables is reserved for Sunday lunch when there is time to enjoy it. And so is the sweet dish or fruit tart that follows the cheese.

The art of balancing a menu is instinctive in a French cook. Not for her guests the huge cream gâteau served in the wake of a cream-bound sauce and an egg and cream thickened soup. No, not even the most important occasion would she celebrate with such an assault on the digestion, as many of her imitators do. She has culinary principles which remain inviolate.

Though customs change with time, inborn characteristics do not. Consequently when the farmer's daughter starts to plan her menus to suit her city life, and diet-conscious generation, she uses her mother's recipes but in different sequences and combinations.

Spring Lunch Menu

Pâté d'Olives (page 28)

•

Fouace aux Herbes (page 36)
Lettuce and Watercress Salad
Vinaigrette dressing (page 13)

•

Mousse Glacée au Rhum (page 90)